Why
BLACK MEN
Jump the Fence?

Real Stories of Why Black Men
Date or Marry Outside of
Their Race

GABRIEL WOODHOUSE

authorHOUSE®

AuthorHouse™
1663 Liberty Drive
Bloomington, IN 47403
www.authorhouse.com
Phone: 1 (800) 839-8640

Published by AuthorHouse 01/03/2018

ISBN: 978-1-5462-2196-8 (sc)
ISBN: 978-1-5462-2194-4 (hc)
ISBN: 978-1-5462-2195-1 (e)

Library of Congress Control Number: 2017919290

Print information available on the last page.

Any people depicted in stock imagery provided by Thinkstock are models, and such images are being used for illustrative purposes only. Certain stock imagery © Thinkstock.

This book is printed on acid-free paper.

Because of the dynamic nature of the Internet, any web addresses or links contained in this book may have changed since publication and may no longer be valid. The views expressed in this work are solely those of the author and do not necessarily reflect the views of the publisher, and the publisher hereby disclaims any responsibility for them.

Kinga James Version (KJV)
Scriptures are taken from the King James Version of The Bible-Public Domain.

Table of Contents

ACKNOWLEDGEMENT   1
DEDICATION   3
FOREWORD   5
INTRODUCTION   7

Root of Colorism   11

Background on Marriages   13
  What is Marriage?   13

Types of Marriages   14
  Interracial Marriage–Biblical Perspective   14
  Interracial Marriage–Legal Perspective   15
  Interracial Marriage–Loving v. Commonwealth of Virginia   15
  Statistics on U.S. Marriages   16

*Background and Commonalities Among the African
American Men Who Date or Marry Outside of Their Race*   21
  Background   21
  Black Men Still Love their Black Women   22
  A Chance Meeting   22
  Negativity   23
  Caters to Their Needs   24
  Physicality   24
  Skin Complexion   25
  Subtle Approach   25
  Selectivity   25
  Feelings of Love and Devotion for their Selected Mate   26

*Real Stories of Why Black Men Jump to Date or Marry
Outside of Their Race*   27
  A Break   27
  Always Positive   30
  Attitude Matters   31
  Awkward Mix   33
  Best Friends   36
  Body Type   39

Childhood Experience 43
Color Complex 45
Comfort Level 46
Country Boy 49
Curiousity 52
Fitness Matters 54
Foreign Interest 56
Fraternity Life 58
Life's Perspective 60
Limited Supply 62
Love Oneself 66
Man Attraction 67
Military Love 70
Mother's Influence 72
My Angel 75
No Animosity 77
Not Black Enough 79
No Depth 81
No Separation 83
Patient Love 86
Pleasantly Surprised 87
Social Connection 90
Spiritual Connection 92
Superficial Mentalities 95
Tickled Fancy 97
Troubled Paradise 99
Turned Off 100
Young Love 103

Real Stories of Why African American Women Jump to Date or Marry White Men 105
Broader Perspective 105
Christian Faith 108
From Then to Now 110

Key Advice from African American Men 113
Attitude 113
Appearance 114
Expectations 114

Friends   115
Secrets   116
Confidence   116

Key Advice from African American Women   117

Advice from a Matchmaker   118
Stage 1   118
Stage 2   118
Stage 3   119
Stage 4   119

Excerpt of Spiritual Advice from a Minister   122
CONCLUSION   125
REFERENCES   127
ABOUT THE AUTHOR   129

ACKNOWLEDGEMENT

As an author, I have been asked quite often by African American women to write a book on "Why African American men date or marry White women." Over the past three years, I pushed this concern of African American women including my wife to the side; but often I wondered whether this book might be helpful to African American women who have the same concern. Maybe this book might be helpful to African American men if African American women knew how they felt. Maybe this book might bring awareness to other races or nationalities. In the words of Maya Angelou's poem the *Human Family*, "we are more alike, my friends, than we are unalike."

As I embarked on this journey, I reminded myself, however, that this does not feel right. I don't want to be perceived as an African American man trying to bring attention to my race and gender. I don't want to be perceived as an African American man trying to start a "feud" between White women and African American women; African American men and African American women; White men and African American men; or White men and White women. Once I started writing the book, I began to think that maybe people will see the value of the book and use it to strengthen their relationships with all people regardless of their race, gender or martial status.

I would like to thank my wife for being the editor for the book. Her continued contribution to my work is paramount. I would like to thank all of the participants who shared their stories about dating and marrying individuals of a different race. I would also like to thank a professional matchmaker for allowing me to provide an excerpt of her presentation from a seminar she conducted on a cruise and a minister for allowing me to use excerpts of his sermon on "Finding My Happy Place."

DEDICATION

This book is dedicated to all of my smart, intelligent and beautiful nieces and single cousins and other African American women who feel that they need to "get in the game" to date and marry African American men or other men of their own interests.

It is my hope that this book will serve as a means to improve understanding of "Why African American men date or marry White women" and other women outside of their race. It is also my hope that the book will inspire women of all races and nationalities to feel free to date whomever they choose without compromising their lifestyles or standards to do so.

FOREWORD

In the early 1990's there was a popular movie titled, "White Men Can't Jump." The implication was that White men did not have the skill-set to dunk a basketball, so to speak. For this book, the critical question to be asked is, Why do African American men "jump the fence." Why do they date or marry White women and other women outside of their race? Is it because of the White woman's complexion, companionship or stewardship? Is it because of her style, class or culture? Is it because of social media, T.V. or radio? Is it because of the African American man's legal right, upbringing or peer pressure? Quite frankly, is there something that the African American woman is not doing to attract and maintain the relationship with African American men? Is it simply because of the African American woman's complexion or skin color?

We know, historically, that an African American man staring at, gesturing or dating a White woman was unacceptable in society. In 1955, Emmett Till, at age 14, was murdered in Mississippi by a pair of White men for allegedly whistling at a White woman.

We know, historically, interracial marriage was illegal and a crime in the U.S. In 1958, Mildred Jeter, a Black woman and Virginia native married Richard Loving, a White man, in the District of Columbia. While returning to Virginia, the couple was arrested for breaking the state's anti-miscegenation laws. It was not until 1967 that the Supreme Court in the case Loving vs. the Commonwealth of Virginia, ruled that laws against interracial marriage were unconstitutional. This was the same year that Sidney Poitier played in the film "Guess Who's Coming to Dinner," about a Black man planning to marry a White woman.

We know also that marriage was not always entered for the mutual benefit of the wedding couple. For thousands of years, individuals had married to "obtain prominent in-laws, complete business mergers, raise capital, enhance their social status, effect military alliances or to enlarge their family labor force" (Ford, 2012).

Using an interviewing process, this book explores the reasons African American men "jump the fence" to date or marry White women and other women outside of their race. Realizing this is not a statistical study, this book provides an opportunity to understand the perspectives of African American men and understand the common themes surfacing from the interviews. In doing so, the interviews include a relatively small sample of 34 African American men who are dating or married to White women and other women outside of their race. It provides interviews of African American women who are dating or married to White men. It also discusses some advice from a matchmaker, minister and African American men and women regarding this subject matter.

INTRODUCTION

In the past few years, there have been a number of movies and relationship advice books that have purported to guide the Black woman on how to date and marry the Black man. Three of the popular or bestselling books include Steve's Harvey's *Act Like A Lady, Think Like a Man: What Men Really Think About Love, Relationships, Intimacy, and Commitment;* Tyrese Gibson and Rev. Run's *Manology, Secrets of Your Man's Mind Revealed;* and La La Anthony's *The Love Playbook: Rules for Love, Sex, and Happiness* (Christopher, 2015).

Considering the status and popularity of these celebrity authors, relationship advice books can have a deleterious influence on how some Black women might change their behavior to satisfy or meet the needs of their mates in order to have and maintain a successful relationship. For instance, some Black women might become totally submissive to their mates in their speech and behavior. Some might attempt to even understand the psyche of their mates, and cater to them accordingly (Christopher, 2015). As many Black women can confess, the sacrifice of this behavior is counterproductive especially when their mates provide little or no love and affection in return. The sacrifice of this behavior is counterproductive when their mates decide to "jump the fence" and date and marry outside of their race.

Since the 1967 Supreme Court decision in the Loving v. Virginia case that invalidated laws to prohibit interracial marriages, people have had the freedom and civil right to date and marry whomever they chose. After the decision, an increase in interracial marriages surfaced throughout the U.S. followed by movies and songs. Currently, a number of T.V. shows such as Scandal, Pitch, Rosewood, and even Black-ish have cast roles with people of different races dating or marrying their counterparts.

Adding to the insurgence of interracial marriages, we now see a number of entertainers and professional athletes forming unions with women of difference races: They include John Legend and Cristine Teigen; Dr. Dre and Nicole Threatt Young; Reggie Bush and Lilit Avagyan; Ellen Pompeo and Chris Ivery; Wesley Snipes and Nikki Park; Michael Jordan and Yvette Prieto; Sidney Poitier and Joanna Shimkus; James Earl Jones and Cecilia Hart; and Cuba Godding Jr. and Sara Kapfer, to name a few.

Enhancing the possibility of dating or marrying, a non-traditional method of selecting a mate has evolved to Internet dating services. These Internet sites give people a larger selection of individuals to date and weed out other people they feel are not dating or marriage potential. Some examples include BlackPeopleMeet. com; eHarmony.com; Match.com and OurTime.com.

Given past and present situations on relationships, it has become apparent that Black women are in a precarious position with regard to dating and marrying Black men. As noted in the 2011 film *Dark Girls*, Black women are confronted with a "deep-seated bias" within their culture due to their dark skin or complexion (See excerpt of film in Figure 1). They get frequently teased and treated unfairly by people in their own race. In addition, according to research by OK Cupid, an online dating site, "Black women are considered the least desired ethnic group by men of all races in America" (found in Kaufman, D., 2017).

Black men are not the only gender who have decided to "jump the fence." Black women, including those in the entertainment industry, have already begun to date or marry outside of their race. They include interracial marriages of Tara Wilson and Chris North in 2012; Janet Jackson and Wissam Al Mana in 2012; Tina Turner and Erwin Bach in 2013; Vanessa Williams and Jim Skrip in 2015; and Serena Williams and Alexis Ohanian in 2017. Adding to the decision to "jump the fence," Malia Obama, former first daughter and freshman at Harvard University, was snapped by the paparazzi kissing a White boy who is a sophomore at Harvard. This book also provides several examples of why African American women chose to date or marry outside of their race.

Figure 1
Excerpt of Film, Dark Girls
(Berry & Duke, 2011)

Root of Colorism

The 2011 film, *Dark Girls* "explores a deep-seated bias within Black culture against women with darker skin." The following provides an excerpt of some key points highlighted in the film:

1. Colorism is "prejudice or discrimination based on the relative lightness or darkness of skin; it is generally a phenomenon occurring with one's own ethnic group."
2. During slavery, light complexion of a slave played a role in the preferential treatment of some Blacks by their slave owners.
3. After slavery, skin color continued to have a deleterious influence on how Blacks are mistreated by Whites, as well as how Black women are mistreated by their own race, particularly Black men.
4. Some Black women are angry about their dark skin color because of how society has promoted dark skin to be ugly and bad.
5. Some Black women hated to have a child of darker complexion because of the stereotype.
6. The impact of skin color on Black women and other women outside of the Black culture is seen as a universal and global problem.
7. Some Black men prefer dating light complexioned women because of pressure from their relatives such as parents and siblings.
8. Some White men praise the looks of Black women including their skin color.

9. The negative images of Blacks on T.V. and the lack of positive images of Blacks in books have added to the stigmatization and negative perception of Blacks.
10. Everything black seems bad such as a funeral; everything white seems good such as a wedding.
11. There is a need for the Black man and woman to discuss the problem of skin color for healing.
12. Blacks were stigmatized by the "paper bag test" whereas beauty was represented by a light complexion and ugliness was represented by a dark complexion.
13. Skin bleaching products are being advertised on T.V. and other mediums as an intervention for Black women to get lighter in order to look white. In 2008, sales of skin bleaching products worldwide increased from $40 to $43 billion.
14. Colorism is perpetuated in society through commercials, movies, and magazines.

Background on Marriages

The following sections provide an understanding of marriages including types of marriages and interracial marriages.

What is Marriage?

Marriage, known as a wedlock or matrimony, is a ritually or socially "recognized union between spouses that establishes rights and obligations between" themselves, their children and in-laws (Wikipedia).

Types of Marriages

While people get married for various reasons such as raising a family and economic security, there are several types of marriages. These include monogamy, serial and polygamy. Monogamy is a marriage with one person. Serial is marriage with a different person after a divorce or death of the first spouse. Polygamy is a marriage in which a person marries two or more individuals at a time, but this type of marriage is illegal in the U.S. (Wikipedia).

Interracial Marriage–Biblical Perspective

Many individuals in the bible such as Moses and Ruth married outside of their race. Moses, a Jew, married an Ethiopian woman outside of his tribe. Moses' siblings, Miriam and Aaron, criticized him for such marriage; and they were confronted by God.

Ruth, a Moabite woman, married into an Israelite family and adopted the faith of her family. After the death of her Israelite husband, she traveled to Israel with her mother-in-law and married a wealthy man, named Boaz.

For God said (1 Corinthians, 7: 8-9), "It is better to marry than burn." God also said, (2 Corinthians, 6:14), "Be ye not unequally yoked together with unbelievers" (King James Bible).

Interracial Marriage—Legal Perspective

Interracial marriage is considered a marriage between spouses outside their race. According to the U.S. Census Bureau, there are approximately 6.9 percent interracial married couples in America (Brown, 2013). Historically, anti-miscegenation laws prohibited interracial marriage. Depending on the state, these laws criminalized sex and cohabitation of Whites and non-whites particularly Blacks. These laws were established in Maryland and Virginia as early as the 1660s. Many U.S. states continue to enforce prohibitions against interracial marriage, despite numerous repeals in the 19th century. In the Perez v. Sharp case (1948), the California Supreme Court ruled California's anti-miscegenation statute unconstitutional. Relying partially on the Perez v. Sharp case, the Supreme Court in the Loving v. Commonwealth of Virginia case (1967) ruled laws against interracial marriage or anti-miscegenation were unconstitutional, overruling the Pace v. Alabama case in 1883 (Wikepedia).

Interracial Marriage—Loving v. Commonwealth of Virginia

This landmark case involves Virginians Mildred Jeter, a Black woman and Richard Loving, a White man. In Virginia, the anti-miscegenation statute and the Racial Integrity Act of 1924, "prohibited marriage between people classified as "white" and people classified as "colored." Despite the state's statute, the couple married in the District of Columbia. Once the Lovings returned to Virginia, they were arrested and sentenced to one year in prison for breaking the state's anti-miscegenation statute. The Lovings, however, were offered the chance of not serving the sentence if they left Virginia and did not return to the state as a couple for 25 years.

Contrary to the statute, the Lovings left the state but returned to visit family members. Once authorities discovered them, they were arrested again for violating the statue. In an attempt to gain their freedom, the Lovings appealed the charges all the way to the Supreme Court. Subsequently, the highest Court of the land ruled in 1967 that the state's anti-miscegenation laws violated the Equal Protection Clause of the Fourteenth Amendment. As a basic civil right, the Court stated that, "The Fourteenth Amendment requires that the freedom of choice to marry not be restricted by invidious racial discrimination. Under our Constitution, the freedom to marry, or not marry, a person of another race resides with the individual and cannot be infringed by the State" (Wikipedia).

Statistics on U.S. Marriages

The following provides some statistics of all Americans in the U.S. and, particularly, Black women in America.

1. In their lifetime, it is projected that 85% of all Americans will marry; from their first marriage, 40% will depart in a divorce and successive marriages resulting at a 60% and 70% rate respectively (Campbell & Wright found in, Liu, 2016).
2. It is reported that "41.9% of Black women in America have never been married" compared to 21.7% of White women; "Black women are the least coupled group in the U.S." (Berry & Duke, 2011).
3. "By 1950, 64% of all Black women were married, roughly the same percentage of White women," and they were roughly the same age; By 1970, the number of Black women marrying by age 29 years dropped by 25% compared to 13% for White women; and the overall rate of Black women never marrying has doubled compared to White women from 5% to 10% (Liu, 2016).
4. It is estimated that "1 in every 3 Black women over the age of 30 will never marry" (Schnieder found in Liu, 2016).
5. "Today, 70% of Black women are unmarried and are twice as likely as White women to remain unwed. Of those who

do marry, Black women are more likely to "marry down" as Black women in college today outnumber Black men 2:1. The unemployment rate for Black men over age 20 years is 17% (Bolick found in Lius, 2016).

6. In America, approximately 6.9% of married couples are interracial; the percentage in Washington, D.C. is approximately 11% (Brown, 2013).

7. In 1960, there were approximately 51,000 White-Black, interracial married couples. Of this number, 25,000 consisted of a White woman and a Black man. In 1980, there were approximately 167,000 White-Black, interracial married couples. Of this number, 122,000 consisted of a White woman and a Black man. In 1997, there were approximately 311,000 White-Black, interracial married couples. Of this number, 201,000 consisted of a White woman and Black man; and 110,000 consisted of a White man and Black woman. In 2002, there were approximately, 395,000 White-Black, interracial married couples. Of this number, 279,000 consisted of a White woman and Black man; and 116,000 consisted of a White man and Black woman (U.S. Census Bureau found in Wright, 2006).

8. In 2009, there were approximately 354,000 White woman and Black man interracial married couples. Of this number, 196,000 consisted of a White man and Black woman (U.S. Census Bureau, 2009).

9. In 2010, 168,000 Black women were married to a White husband, 4,072,000 to a Black husband, 9,000 to an Asian husband and 18,000 to other husband. In the same year, 50,410,000 White women were married to a White husband, 390,000 to a Black husband, 219,000 to an Asian husband and 488,000 to other husband (Wikipedia).

10. Approximately 15% of first time marriages in the U.S. in 2010 were between couples from a different race compared to 6.7% in 1980. For all marriages in the same year, 8.4%

were couples from a different race compared to 3.2 in 1980 (Pew Research Center, 2012).

11. In 2013, approximately 12% of first time marriages in the U.S. were between newlyweds of different races (Pew Research Center, 2015).

12. In 2015, approximately 10% of all marriages in the U.S. were between people of a different ethnicity or race compared to 3% in 1980. In the same year, 17% of all weddings performed were interracial compared to 7% in 1980 (Pew Research Center found in Balwit, 2017).

13. In 2015, "18% of new marriages in metropolitan areas were interracial compared to 11% of newlyweds outside of metropolitan areas." Figure 2 provides the percentage of the newlyweds who are married to people of a different ethnicity or race in the top 10 metropolitan areas (Pew Research Center found in Balwit, 2017).

14. In 2015, newlywed intermarriages were 17% compared to 3% in 1967 after the Loving v. Virginia case (Pew Research Center found in Livingston, G. & Brown, A., 2017).

15. In 2015, newlywed intermarriages for Asians were 29% compared to Hispanics 27%; Blacks 18% and White 11% (Pew Research Center found in Livingston, G. & Brown, A., 2017).

16. In 2015, newlywed intermarriages for White men were 12% compared to 10% for White women; newlywed intermarriages for Black men were 24% compared to 12% for Black women; newlywed intermarriages for Hispanic men were 26% compared to 28% for Hispanic women; newlywed intermarriages for Asian men were 21% compared to 36% for Asian women (Pew Research Center found in Livingston, G. & Brown, A., 2017). Figure 3 provides an overall percentage of U.S. newlyweds (interracial marriages) along with a breakdown by ethnic groups in 2015.

Figure 2
% of U.S. Newlyweds (Interracial Marriages)
in Top 10 Metropolitan Areas, 2015

Top 10	Percentage
Honolulu, Hi	42%
Las Vegas-Henderson-Paradise, NV	31%
Santa Maria-Santa Barbara, CA	30%
Fayetteville, NC	29%
Palm Bay-Melbourne-Titusville, FL	29%
Albuquerque, NM	28%
Stockton-Lodi, CA	28%
Anchorage, AK	28%
Ogden-Clearfield, UT	27%
San Diego-Carlsbad, CA	27%

Bottom 10	
Greensboro-High Point, NC	9%
Scranton-Wilkes-Barre-Hazleton, PA	9%
Lafayette, LA	9%
Baton Rouge, LA	8%
Birmingham-Hoover, AL	6%
Greenville-Anderson-Mauldin, SC	6%
Chattanooga, TN-GA	5%
Youngstown-Warren-Boardman, OH-PA	4
Asheville, NC	3%
Jackson, MS	3%

Figure 3
% of U.S. Newlyweds (Interracial Marriages) in 2015

Overall %	Ethnic Group %	
Asian 29%		
	Asian Men 21%	Asian Women 36%
Hispanic 27%		
	Hispanic Men 26%	Hispanic Women 28%
Black 18%		
	Black Men 24%	Black Women 12%
White 11%		
	White Men 12%	White Women 10%

For this book, the critical question to be asked is: "Why do African American men "jump the fence" to date or marry White women and other women outside of their race? Through interviews, this book seeks to answer the question. The interviews include a relatively small sample of 34 African American men who are dating or married to White women and other women outside of their race. These men, however, were raised and currently reside in different parts of the United State. Additionally, this book provides several interviews of African American women who are dating or married to White men. Finally, it discusses advice from African American men and women, a matchmaker and minister related to this subject matter. For confidentiality, the names of the interviewees have been changed.

Background and Commonalities Among the African American Men Who Date or Marry Outside of Their Race

Background

The African American men represented in this book were reared and currently reside in different parts of the United States. They come from the states of Arizona, Arkansas, Florida, Georgia, California, Illinois, Mississippi, Michigan, New Jersey, New York, Oklahoma, Texas, Virginia and Washington. The majority of the men were from two parent households that have significantly lengthy marriages. Others were from divorced families.

The men work in occupations such as education, the military and entertainment (acting and National Football League). They work in fields such as management and healthcare. They also work in various industries doing blue collar work or operating their own businesses. While most of the men were raised in the Baptist faith, many of them were not actively involved in the church. The interviewees ranged in age from 19–67. Their relationships comprised of mostly White women; however, there were some who were in active relationships with Asians, Brazilians, Hispanics, Mexicans and Turkish women.

Regarding education, the interviewees all had a high school degree with others securing college degrees. Their mates were often similarly degreed.

The objective of the interviews was to gain a better understanding of why Black Men choose to date and marry outside of their race. Below are the collective learnings garnered from the interviews.

Black Men Still Love their Black Women

Black Men overwhelmingly agreed that even though they were dating and marrying White women and other women outside of their race, they still love their Black women. They described Black women as strong and being the backbone of the family. They respect Black women for the strength they display and acknowledged that Black women have been molded by history to stand up and be strong. As one interviewee put it, all he has known is Black women and has been raised by a strong Black woman. Another interviewee explained it this way, "I love their dark complexion, full lips and short natural hair. Black women are everything to me." See the stories—Spiritual Connection, Awkward Mix and Attitude Matters—for a more thorough discussion.

A Chance Meeting

The majority of the interviewees indicated that they were not actively looking to date outside of their race. They were introduced to their acquaintances through various means. Some met the women through mutual friends, at work, school or at a social event; and one interviewee indicated the meeting occurred due to their children. It was clear that it was proximity that opened the door to building a relationship with a woman outside of their race. As one interviewee put it, "I just didn't wake up one day and want to date outside my race, it just happened." A few connected on social media (a rarity); and at least one interviewee indicated there was curiosity about White women even though he had been coached by his mother to not date White women. In the story on "Curiosity," Oliver Johnston said, he had always been curious about White women but the chance had never presented itself until a particular social event. Additionally, he wasn't sure how to approach his White girl friend or how to start the conversation. However, to his delight once the conversation began, they had a lot in common. Another interviewee said he was ready to experience something different. He said he had a "bad run" with Black women and wanted to try an interracial relationship. See article on No Separation for further discussion about chance meeting.

Negativity

The strong Black woman comes with a strong attitude. Many of the men indicated that they are pushed away from Black women because of this attitude. They described the attitudes as "angry, frustrated and confrontational." In the following story on "A Break," Jeremy Johnson said, Black women have a different view of what being a man is, they start off with the negative. White women don't come with all the baggage. You're a man and it doesn't have to be proven. And, it's not that it's easier to be with a White woman, but nothing is under the microscope. White women might do a checklist on what type of person you are, but it's not a checklist of your manhood. But with Black women, it seems to be a checklist that adds up to if you're a man or not. There's no tug of war with White women. There's no limbo to see whose womanhood or manhood wins with White women. See more on negativity in the articles—Comfort Level, Love Oneself, Man Attraction, Best Friends, Color Complex, Foreign Interests and Pleasantly Surprised.

Caters to Their Needs

In the following story on "Country Boy," Rodney Foster said, he would "bust his butt" for his White girl friend because she totally cares about him and is sensitive to his needs. She gives him a manicure and pedicure and makes breakfast and lunch for him; whereas, his former African American wife and other African American women did not do those things for him. Another interviewee shared how he initially felt uncomfortable letting his Mexican girl friend fix his plate. He later learned this was a cultural thing which he never experienced with his former African American wife. Another interviewee described his White mate as being more patient while another described his mate as being "loyal through many difficult times." In the story, "My Angel," Grant talked about how his mate came into his life while dealing with legal issues and described her as his angel who embraced him as he was. See articles on Patient Love, Pleasantly Surprised and Superficial Mentalities for more discussion on catering to the Black man's needs.

Physicality

While several of the men indicated that they are not bothered by different sizes of African American women, there were a number of the interviewees with significant concerns about how these women cared for their weight and health. In the following story on "Body Type," Cleve Rogers said, many African American women undermine the value of staying fit to maintain a nice body type and stamina for sexual intimacy. They start off in the relationship with good intentions but become very complacent or comfortable with gaining weight, losing their shape and, subsequently, losing interest in sexual intercourse with their man. African American women fail to realize that if an African American man is attracted to their body type, they should at least try to maintain such appearance to the best of their ability according to Rogers. See articles on Fitness

Matters, Body Type and Life's Perspective for more discussion on Physicality.

Skin Complexion

Many of the men had no issues with women of different complexions or hair type or styles. The men stated that they did not mind women wearing weaves but more importantly, they wanted the women to be comfortable with themselves. On a few occasions, men gravitated to White women and had issues with color. For example in the story on "Color Complex," Josh Bird said, he has always been attracted to lighter complexioned women. He has never met a dark-skinned woman that was pretty to him. Darker women can be fine or sexy, but not pretty to him. Lighter complexion women have always been more attractive, said Josh.

Subtle Approach

In the following story on "No Depth," Joshua Hinton said, he isn't interested in women who pursues too strong, but prefers a woman who is somewhat subtle. White women are not as aggressive and boisterous. They tend to be more submissive. And, they don't ask for much, just company.

Selectivity

In the following story on "Limited Supply," Peter Knight said, African American women are too selective or particular in choosing an African American man and this subsequently leaves them being without a man. They set their standards too high and undermine the value of a man who is a blue-collar worker such as a UPS employee. They have high expectation, whereas the White woman has no expectation.

Feelings of Love and Devotion for their Selected Mate

During the interviews, the tones and expressions of the African American men were quite evident of their feelings for their loved ones. They candidly expressed their passion and love for their mates despite the numerous challenges of being in an interracial relationship. They also appeared to be equally yoked with each other resembling various expressions from songs such as "Level" by Stokley Williams. The following are some of the lyrics to "Level."

"Level"

You're never judgmental, judgmental
You build me up and never tear me down
Put you first and never in the background
Lovin' you is simple (simple)
So simple (so simple)
You my shady spot on sunny days
You're summer to my ocean waves
Been waitin' all my life, waitin' all my life

Real Stories of Why Black Men Jump to Date or Marry Outside of Their Race

African American men are dating or marrying outside of their race at a rate significantly higher than African American women are dating or marrying outside of their race. In 2010, for example, 390,000 Black men were married to White women compared to 168,000 Black women married to White men in the same year. To answer the critical question for this book, the following provides an except of interviews from various African American men to explore why African American men "jump the fence" to date or marry outside of their race. For confidentiality, the names have been changed.

A Break

Jeremy Johnson is a 35 year-old single African American man; he has never been married. Both of his parents are African American. They are divorced, and his father is deceased. He is a Baptist Christian and was born in a city in Texas. He has three children. His girlfriend, Laura, was also born in Texas. She is a 27 year-old White woman. They have no kids together. Laura also has no children. Jeremy has an associate's degree, and Laura has a high school diploma.

Jeremy met Laura through a mutual friend. One of Laura's friends was dating a friend of Jeremy's, and they were connected through the friendships. Jeremy explains that there would be nothing that would totally stop him from dating Black women. It's nothing that one Black woman could do, that would make me not be interested in Black women, says Jeremy. I love Black women too much. I don't know that I could be with a White woman for the rest of my life, says Jeremy. Black women will always be around, he says.

Jeremy talks very seriously about his love for Black women. I just love Black women. I love their dark complexion, full lips and particularly short natural hair. Black women are everything to me. I love them, says Jeremy. As for as body type, Jeremy says he likes them fine. I love the Black woman's curves too, says Jeremy.

Jeremy spoke candidly about the differences he has noticed about the two races. What I've noticed is that with White women, man is a state of being. But, with Black women it's more of a state of doing. White women come into the relationship respecting your position and authority as a man, Jeremy explains. Black women tend to or try to challenge you. To make you earn that, it's like you have to earn a position as the man. But with a White woman, you come into that role at the beginning. It's not a challenge or competition, explains Jeremy.

I would never marry a White woman, says Jeremy. Jeremy freely admits that he could never be fully faithful to a White woman. And, my dating a White woman now, isn't an indictment on Black women; it's just somebody that I like. But it absolutely has nothing to do with Black women, Jeremy says.

Jeremy explains that if he's to be approached by a woman, he likes a subtle and focused pursuit, and not too aggressive sexually.

Jeremy further discusses the difference between the races. He has noticed that Black women are more challenging of manhood. They have a different view of what being a man is, they start off with the negative. White women don't come with all the baggage. You're a

man, and it doesn't have to be proven, says Jeremy. And, it's not that it's easier to be with a White woman, but nothing is under the microscope, he says. White women might do a checklist on what type of person you are, but it's not a checklist of your manhood. But with Black women, it seems to be a checklist that adds up to if you're a man or not. There's no tug of war with White women. Like, there's no limbo to see whose womanhood or manhood wins with White women, Jeremy continues to explain. A man falls short with a White woman based solely on what type of person he is; there's no scrutiny like it is with Black women, Jeremy says.

Communication is key to Jeremy. What works in a relationship is communication. You have to be trusted regardless. Open lines of communication, says Jeremy.

Jeremy said he doesn't experience many challenges or barriers in his relationship. He doesn't have any problems when going out either. Societal pressures do not faze him too much. He's not bothered by the thoughts of others. But, just like there are different kinds of Blacks, there are different kinds of Whites. We share the same interests and like the same things. We aren't too far off from each other, Jeremy explains. I haven't felt like I've entered into a whole new world with my White girlfriend. So, no real barriers or challenges exist for me, Jeremy shares.

Traits that I look for are integrity, the type of parent she is, if she has kids, what type of person she is, and how she treats people. I also want to know what her heart is like, or her relationship with her family and friends. These are all important traits Jeremy looks for in a mate.

Advice Jeremy gives to Black women regarding maintaining a positive relationship with a Black man is to chill out! Just chill out, he said. Everything isn't the end of the world. Black women are too uptight sometimes, Jeremy exclaims.

Always Positive

Sheldon Carr is a 31-year old African American man from a city in Texas. He's never been married. Both of his parents are African American. The two of them never married and are both currently single. He considers himself a Baptist Christian.

Sheldon is dating Tenea Garcia, a Hispanic woman. Tenea is 32 years-old and is also from Texas. The two of them have two children together. Tenea has one child from a previous relationship. Sheldon works at a freight company, and is working toward completing his CDL license to drive trucks locally for his company. Tenea manages a temp agency. The two of them met when they were 19.

Sheldon said he saw Tenea coming out of a gas station and decided to approach her. They dated a short while before their first child was born. Sheldon has dated African American women. He said he loves African American women and prefers them. He even feels like he's more comfortable with them. I just didn't wake up one day and want to date outside my race; it just happened, he said. He explained that he and Tenea clicked, and once their son was born, he was all in. He explained that he's the type of man that doesn't run from responsibility. He wants to be a father to his children.

Some of the challenges he finds are how the two of them were raised. He was raised by a single African American woman and was taught to do everything in his household; whatever I was told to do, I had to do it, said Sheldon. However, Tenea was raised in a household where her father took care of the household bills, and her mom and siblings stayed home. This is crippling for kids, I think, said Sheldon. I know it crippled her, he said. It's 2017, and I just think today we're better off if everybody chips in. Sometimes she expects me to do everything, and I'm not feeling that, Sheldon said.

Sheldon said he prefers whatever hair style that makes a woman feel most comfortable. He talked about how he's not a fan of relaxed hair. He mentioned a time where his niece had such beautiful hair before she put a relaxer in it, and the negative impact the chemicals had on her hair. Confidence shows in a woman's character, he said. And, that's what attracts me to a woman, said Sheldon.

One reservation he has about African American women is the lack of femininity. He said the young women try hard to be more like a man, or more hardcore. He said that's not attractive. But, there's a lack of good African American men in the Black community, so he understands the frustration of African American women.

Moreover, Sheldon said he likes women that are confident and are comfortable being themselves. Like the song says, "Ain't got a type, I just like what I like, he said. Or, just a woman that can hold her own. He explained that maintaining a level of positivity is the most important aspect of his relationship. I choose to maintain a positive relationship, he said. Regardless of what's happening, I keep positive at all times. It's for my kids, he said. Kids pick up on all that's going on, so I try to remain positive around them, said Sheldon.

The advice Sheldon gives to African American women is to be encouraged and set goals with your man. Know where you want to be in ten years, and try to reach milestones with the man you are with. Instead of just being focused on having a good time, get to know what he wants out of life and compare his wants and goals to yours. Sheldon said, he wants somebody that's the opposite of a killjoy. He wants a woman who is not so angry or frustrated; somebody that's open-minded and interested in building a solid future.

Attitude Matters

Lester Long is a 34 year-old single African American man from a city in Texas. Both of Lester's parents are African American. His father is deceased, and his mother is currently married. Geri is a 31 year-old Asian woman from a city in Texas. Geri grew up nondenominational, but converted to Christianity when she began dating Lester. Geri is a stay-at-home Mom, and Lester owns a construction company. The two of them have three children together, but have never married.

Lester stated that he met Geri through a mutual friend. They talked quite a lot on the phone before actually meeting in person at a local park in Texas. At first, she wasn't what I expected. I actually thought she was a Black woman and was turned off that she was not Black, stated Lester. I really didn't think we would talk anymore, Lester explained. The relationship, however, did continue after that meet and greet in the park. They've now been dating for over ten years.

In the past, I've dated Black women. I've always loved Black women and that there are no factors that led him away from them, stated Lester. I love women with a good attitude, smart and know how to speak correctly. None of the physical stuff really matters to me that much, said Lester. She just has to be smart, have a good attitude, be cool, and have something going for herself, Lester said. Lester elaborated on the point that, physical qualities are fleeting, but intellect and attitude or perspective is everlasting.

Lester explained the relationship with Geri moved extremely fast. She was pregnant within a short period of time, which forced him to take care of his family. In the relationship, Lester explained that he loves to cook, and that it's become one of his passions. He cooks every night for his family, and it never seems like a chore; he emphasized that Geri is not one that enjoys cooking, but that it doesn't bother him because he enjoys it so much. He said if ever he were to be approached by a woman, he'd want her to offer him a dinner date.

As a couple, Lester said that they were pretty much the same; Geri was kind of like a Black girl, said Lester. I can't really see any differences that I noticed. We like most of the same stuff, he said. One of the main challenges in the relationship was Geri's family. Geri and Lester had their first baby right out of high school. Once Geri got pregnant, her parents disowned her. Lester explained it was because he's a Black man. He explained that Geri's parents took everything from her, and wouldn't allow her back in their home. Lester had no choice but to move Geri in with him, and prepare for their family. Geri's father still does not talk to me after 10 years, said Lester. Lester described a time when he tried sitting next to Geri's father and initiated conversation at a family cookout; however, Geri's father immediately got up, and sat somewhere else. Lester firmly believes that race is the factor; however, explained that her parents treat their three girls without any discrimination.

While in the public, Lester talked about being judged primarily by Black women; he always felt judged, or as if they looked at him funny. He attributed it to their just not knowing the person that he is; he said the people that actually know him, understood his reasons for dating outside his race, and appreciate the person that he is.

Lester's advice to women is to be independent, but let a man be a man. Lester elaborated by saying this doesn't mean women need to "be bare foot and pregnant in a kitchen," but simply should step back and allow a man to take care of the household.

Awkward Mix

Tony Baker is a 39 year-old African American man. He was married for three years to an African American woman. Both of his parents are African American and have been married for 40 years. Tony is a Baptist Christian. He was born in a city in Illinois. His current girlfriend is an African American woman, however, he co-parents two children with Sara, whom is a 38 year old White woman. Sara was born in a city in Arizona. Tony has six of his own children and two with Sara. Tony drives trucks locally in the Illinois area.

Tony met Sara on a popular street people frequent on the weekends in Arizona. Tony said Sara approached and pursued him that night. They hit it off pretty quickly, he said. All my life, I grew up hearing not to date White women, said Tony. Tony explained that his mother was adamant about his not dating women outside of the African American race. Most of his life, he only dated Black women; he explained he had no interest initially in dating a White woman, but did grow increasingly curious about other races as he got older.

Tony said there were no factors that led him away from Black women. All, I've ever known is Black women, strong Black women too. I was raised by strong Black women, he said. Black women are the backbone of the household and families. Tony said he's attracted to all types of women. He has no particular hair style, body size, or physical characteristic that he prefers. As I've gotten older, I've started to pay more attention to who the woman is. Is she family oriented? Is she a people person? How does she feel about kids? Was her father in her life? These are characteristics and questions Tony said are important to him, and what he believes is what attracts him to a woman.

Tony said he has no reservations about Black women, but if you flip the question, I do have reservations about White women, he said. I wish I would've known then, what I know now about interracial relationships. For example, there are a lot of compromises that I never considered, like music selections, food, and the holidays with families. There are explanations about life and being Black in America that I have to explain to my children with Sara, that I don't have to explain to my children that aren't bi-racial, he explained.

Tony said he was never seeking to date outside his race, but while living in Arizona, there weren't many Black people to choose from, he explained. Tony admitted he didn't particularly care for dating outside his race. He actually often times felt embarrassed when out in public with Sara. I've never been the type of guy to say I want to date a White woman; I was curious though, he said.

Tony talked about the holidays, and how his and Sara's family didn't mix very well. It was always awkward, Tony explained. I remember food being a simple but most difficult compromise. White people eat stuffing on Thanksgiving, we eat dressing, he said. I don't eat pumpkin pie, but Sara had never eaten sweet potato pie, Tony said. These simple differences made a big difference in the levels of comfortability, Tony explained.

Tony said that comprise and sacrifice are the two most important factors that contribute to maintaining positive relationships. The ability to not be selfish, he said. I'm used to Black women, so it was an adjustment for me, said Tony. I had to learn to take into consideration a new way of thinking and a different culture when being with a White woman.

The barrier that Tony found to be most challenging is explaining to his children the differences between being raised as a Black child in comparison to being raised as a White child. Sara will never be able to explain the challenges of Black people to my children, he explained. My kids are oblivious to the struggle I experience as a Black man in my daily life. Tony talked about having to also explain to his daughters why their physical features were bigger than their mom's. He said his daughter didn't understand why her hair was curly and not straight like her mom's hair. And, why her feet were big. Tony said he talks to his daughters about the features that they've inherited genetically from his side of the family, and why they are different. This can be a difficult conversation sometimes, he said.

Tony said he likes women that are outgoing and family oriented. He wants them to love children and have a desire to travel. Tony said that the advice he'd give a woman is to stand by your man, be supportive, be trusting and trustworthy, be open to try new things and learn to agree to disagree.

Best Friends

Teenagers who date and marry the same person early in their life may become curious to meet and date someone else later in life. Gabriel Hosendorf, a native of Mississippi, started dating his African American girlfriend when he was in the 7th grade; and they got married immediately after graduating from high school. She was his high school sweetheart, says Hosendorf.

Although they were happily married for 15 years and had three children, Hosendorf said their curiosity got the best of them. They peacefully divorced "to determine what other people were like in the world. They both wanted to see what life was about beyond the two of them." At the same time, they remained "best friends" and still are "best friends" today, says Hosendorf.

As part of Hosendorf's assessing what other people were like in the world, he dated different women including his 2nd wife, a White woman who he met in Illinois and was married to her for a short period of time. Because of irreconcilable differences, the marriage ended. Thereafter, Hosendorf met another White woman, a native of Tennessee, at his job in Illinois. He talked to her for six months in a professional manner before asking her out on a date. They dated for three years, and Hosendorf allowed her to move in with him when she got laid off from work. Currently, they have been happily married for six years.

While they do not have any children together, Hosendorf said that he was attracted to his third wife, a White woman, because of her personality, intelligence, creativity and sensitivity to his needs. He was also attracted to her because she was trustworthy, genuine, caring and honest. She treated him very special during the dating period and remained attentive to details throughout their relationship. Her laugh was so adorable, says Hosendorf.

Educationally, Hosendorf and his wife both received high school diplomas. He was employed with a manufacturing company for 37 years in the roles of painter, inspector and supervisor; and his wife was employed as laborer at the same company. They worship together at a Pentecostal Church although Hosendorf was raised Baptist.

While currently retired at 67, Hosendorf expressed that his third wife of age 53 exemplified the same or similar characteristics of his first wife. He said his first wife was well-spoken, quiet, kind and caring. She was well-taught as an African American woman and did not go beyond her boundaries. She was "head and shoulder" over the African American woman of today, says Hosendorf.

Like father like son, Hosendorf's two sons (ages 50 and 39) looked for the same characteristics in a woman. While his sons both dated an African American woman and one even married an African American woman in the past, they both are married to a woman outside of their race (Mexican and White). Hosendorf explained that his sons were disgusted with the African American woman's negative behavior and refused to continue marriage or endure such antics on a daily basis.

Hosendorf's African American daughter (age 40), however, does not have the same views of her African American brothers and father. Hosendorf said she feels compelled to be hard, tough and vociferous and not be in any way submissive to a man. While she dates an African American man, she feels it is her right to be whomever she pleases to be and will not change for anyone. She is going to stand her ground and not take any mess from anybody, says Hosendorf.

When asked how he liked to be pursued by a woman, Hosendorf stated that the woman should show some intelligence, joy and laughter in her personality, carry herself in a lady like fashion, articulate her background to stimulate his interest or curiosity and demonstrate she can be fun around him. Also, she should show that she has a business mindset, can be relationship oriented rather than self-oriented, be supportive when the mate faces adversity and avoid sexual relations immediately while dating. She should preferably get to know me first, says Hosendorf.

While interracial marriages can encounter social challenges, Hosendorf noted that they are well received by their family members, Pentecostal Church members and friends. When they initially visited family members and stayed in hotels, they were told to avoid wasting hotel expenses and stay with their family. In addition, they have not encountered any negative challenges, barriers or prejudices such as being denied access to public settings while being a couple. They have only observed people staring at them.

The Illinois community where they reside and attend church is populated with people of different races, and the people are receptive to their lifestyle. They did, however, question themselves about the marriage when they visited Atlanta and people kept staring and looking at them in a demeaning and displeasing way. They expressed to each other, "What in the world have we gotten ourselves into," says Hosendorf.

When asked the question of about his advice regarding an African American woman who is seeking to date or marry an African American man, Hosendorf's responses were based on his experience being married to his first wife, an African American woman and his current wife a White woman. His responses were also based on his observing the behavior of African American and White women in the public. This was in his role as a part-time traffic monitor and a store assistant. Through hundreds of scenarios, Hosdendorf observed how the African American woman would be very impatient, mean and vociferous toward pedestrians crossing the street at a traffic stop, as well as toward cashiers when purchasing an item from a store. In the same scenarios, he observed how the White woman would be very patient, kind and respectful to the individuals.

As such, Hosendorf advises African American women to take a very good look at themselves on how they behave; relinquish the me, me, me attitude or syndrome; if in a marriage, allow it to be mutual; don't let your demands be all about materialistic things; be reflective in how you got the man and what it takes to keep him; don't change in mid-stream; don't be so loud and vociferous; don't go out in the public trying to be seen by everybody; focus on your man; ask yourself the critical question why African American men are turning to other races; be gentle and kind; don't be confrontational with your man; know, act or play your part in the relationship; be peaceful in your behavior; and don't show it negatively in the public.

Body Type

Staying fit is a good way to maintain a healthy life not only physically, but also sexually, says Cleve Rogers. Many African American women undermine the value of staying fit to maintain a nice body type and stamina for sexual intimacy. They start off in the relationship with good intentions but become very complacent or comfortable with gaining weight, losing their shape and, subsequently, losing interest in sexual intercourse with their man. African American women fail to realize that if an African American man is attracted to their body type, they should at least try to maintain such appearance to the best of their ability, says Rogers.

Roger, (29) who served time in the military, resides in the Midwest with his wife Queen (29) who also served time in the military. They have been married for three years and have one son. Rogers, a college graduate, was raised by two parents who also served time in the military. He had a grandparent who was involved in an interracial marriage. Queen, a college graduate, was raised by two parents with a military background and no interracial couple history.

While Queen, a White woman, never dated outside of her race; she met Rogers on a deployment (plane trip) to South Asia with the conversations taking place for six hours. With limited people to date in this particular region of Asia, Rogers and Queen secretly dated for one year to avoid any potential conflict or drama on the military base. While residing in separate dorms, Rogers sneaked into Queen's dorm to court her.

After Queen became pregnant, the couple decided to move in together at Rogers' place in the U.S. and shortly thereafter married. At first sight, Rogers was attracted to Queen's facial appearance and personality. Queen, however, was hesitant to talk to Rogers and initially hated him before becoming a good friend and forming a serious relationship with him, says Rogers. Being different from most of Rogers' African American girlfriends, Queen takes care of her body by working out four times a week and maintaining a strong interest in sexual intercourse with Rogers. Queen has a remarkable personality, allows Rogers to be himself and allows Rogers to talk to her about anything including his contracting a sexually transmitted disease (STD) in college. Queen also refrains from sharing his personal matters with others people such as her girlfriends. In the early stages of their dating, Queen also did not have a problem with Rogers' harsh looking feet that he significantly bruised from playing recreational basketball, says Rogers.

As happy as this couple's marriage seems, Rogers indicated that there are some challenges they experience from people in the community, particularly White men and African American women. Both sexes give dirty looks and disapproval of Rogers and Queen being together as a couple. They don't say anything or inflict any physical attacks, but their mannerisms are very offensive, annoying and appalling, says Rogers.

With racial tension and social unrest on the rise, Rogers and Queen make the very best of their relationship by having positive discussions on sensitive subject matters (racism, politics, terrorism, religion, etc.) and walking away from the discussion with an understanding of each other's perspectives. Being in an interracial marriage provides a unique advantage and outlet for understanding each race's viewpoints. It is something he could not get outside of his marriage including at work. "The discussions strengthen our marriage," says Rogers. Although Rogers has been trained by an African American police officer on how to conduct himself when stopped by a White police officer such as making sure you are not perceived as a threat to them, Queen wholeheartedly reminds him to make sure he makes it home safely because they have a son to rear together, says Rogers.

Due to immaturity, lack of trust and cheating on each other, Rogers' six-year relationship with an African American woman ended mutually. The girlfriend wanted to experience life which was during the time Rogers was in high school and college. In another African American relationship, the girlfriend's parents had a problem with Rogers' background and light complexion. The parents were from Africa and, culturally, did not see their daughter and Rogers being equally yoked. Another girlfriend treated him like she was his mom, and a final girlfriend would not keep his personal business a secret.

If African American women are wondering why they have a difficult time dating or marrying an African American man and maintaining a positive relationship with them, they should consider a few things, says Rogers. First, African American women should stop thinking that every African American man must fit a certain profile in order to be in a relationship with them. Rogers says because he articulates words very clearly and sounds like a White man, this is a turn off to African American women who he comes in contact with in the community as well as his friends. So, African American women should be open to the African American man's background, history and lifestyle; and allow him to be who he is and not someone else.

Second, whatever attracted you or your mate to the relationship such as physical appearance, maintain that appearance. Find an exercise program that works for you and helps to maintain your health. This helps to stimulate interest and intimacy in the relationship. In essence, you don't want to drive a "tore up car if you can avoid it. It is nicer to drive a new car such as a BMW. You want to show off your wife the same way you show off your car. You want to hear the comments from others that your wife looks great, so don't let your body deteriorate. It may not break or make a relationship, but it can help, says Rogers.

Third, be who you are in the relationship. Don't start adding wigs or artificial hair to look like someone else. Remember, African American women should maintain the same appearance that led the man to being attracted to them. We are looking at their appearance on a daily basis, so don't change and be comfortable with who you are.

Fourth, don't share your man's personal business with your girlfriends. This is very disturbing. No man wants to feel like he is dating you and all of your girlfriends at the same time.

Fifth, remain sexually active in the relationship. Don't forget this is important in a relationship. Be proactive rather than reactive in having sex with your mate. I like spontaneity and an aggressive woman. In fact, I like the way my wife comes home and eagerly states, "It's game time! Let's go!," says Rogers.

Childhood Experience

A person's childhood experience can influence how he or she chooses a friend or mate. Marcus Spencer was raised in small town in Michigan where his industrial community and schools (elementary through high school) were mixed with people from different racial backgrounds and cultures. There were no such things as segregated schools for Blacks and Whites. As such, his best friend was Chinese who enjoyed eating his mother's spaghetti.

While reared by a single parent, worshipping at a Baptist church and being actively involved in the Black Power Movement, Spencer (63) is happily married to a Turkish woman. His current wife (53) was born in Turkey, raised in Germany and practiced an Islamic religion. The couple respects each other's method of worship and attends each other's church together. They have been married for 10 years and have two children together. They each have two additional children from their former marriages.

According to Spencer, he was first married to an African American woman for nine years. He dated other African American women before dating and, subsequently, marrying his current wife. He expressed there were only cultural differences among the women with whom he formed relationships, particularly in terms of how they were raised. Turkish women such as his wife, appear to respect or honor their elders a lot more than African Americans. They also appear to be more sensitive to an African American man's plight, says Spencer.

Ironically, Spencer met his Turkish wife in the Southeast region of the U.S. through their children at their middle and high schools. Since the children were friends and the couple saw each other frequently at school functions, this helped to form a wonderful relationship with them as a couple and family, says Spencer.

Spencer and his wife have not faced any racial tension, barriers or challenges as a married couple. Family members and people in the community respect their rights and privileges as a couple. Considering time has changed and the world is not as taboo as it once was, an unpleasant stare has been the most they experienced from people in the community, says Spencer.

With the rapid increase of police brutality on African American men, Spencer noted that he and his wife voice their disdain about it rather than the matter being a conflict to the marriage. For guidance and understanding, he said they also have frequent conversations with their grown children about the issue. Although many African American men are victimized by police brutality, the violent treatment of law enforcement impacts all people regardless of their race, says Spencer.

While there are numerous factors that contribute to the lack of availability of African American men to date or marry, some African American women feel frustrated about their chances of dating or marrying within their race, especially when they see African American men dating or marrying outside of their race. To give an opinion on how African American women can overcome this dilemma, Spencer stated that the question is too broad to advise women on such matter. He is not an expert on the subject since he did not have a successful marriage to an African American woman. Relationships, nevertheless, are very difficult for people regardless of their race, says Spencer.

In choosing a mate, Spencer indicated that he looks for a woman who is trustworthy, loveable and humble, and someone he could share his life with together and reciprocate the qualities in return.

Color Complex

Josh Bird is a 37 year-old single African American man. Both of his parents are African Americans, and were married to each other during the adolescent stage of his life. His father later remarried, but his mother remained single. Josh and his brother were primarily raised by their mother. They were raised in a Christian Baptist household, and still maintain the same faith and belief in God. Josh, however, is not an active member of a church today. His girlfriend, Jordan, is a 28 year-old White woman. The two of them have no children together, and no children from past relationships. They have been dating for eight years. Josh graduated from a historically Black college; Jordan did not attend college. They both are aspiring actors in California, and met on a set of a movie.

Josh has dated African American women throughout his life; however, he has always been attracted to lighter complexioned women. I have never met a dark-skinned woman that was pretty to me. Darker women can be fine or sexy, but not pretty to him, says Josh. Lighter complexion women have always been more attractive, Josh explains. But, it wasn't the main reason for his dating outside of his race. There was nothing in particular about Black women that caused him to date outside his race. What attracted him to Jordan was her patient way. She accepted his instability. She was sort of a push-over at first, says Josh. But most importantly, she took care of him. That's what made him stay with her. As a struggling actor/entertainer, Josh explains that he needed a supportive woman. He says this type of support and patience, from his experience, wasn't something Black women could offer or understood how to give him.

There's not a particular reservation that I have about Black women, but most of them are feisty and give attitude, says Josh. In the relationship with Jordan, Josh explains that initially she seemed happy to just be with him. And, he even sensed that she sometimes was a little scared of him, which also made her tolerate a lot more than most Black women would tolerate. When he met Jordan, he never really considered dating a White woman, but knew several friends that were or had in the past. The consensus of his friends was that White women took care of their men, and that they had money to create a stable life. This also had an impact on why Josh gave interracial dating a chance, and what led him to date a White woman.

While Josh likes women to approach him subtly, he explains that Black women have less patience, and are hard to deal with at times. White women go with the flow more, and are more accepting. I think the most important part of maintaining a good relationship is communication, regardless of the person's race says Josh. That's all to it.

Further, Josh explains that living in California has lessened the stress that most people may experience in an interracial relationship. People are liberal here. Soon everybody's going to be mixed anyway, at the rate interracial dating is going. I think that's the biggest problem Black people have with it. They feel like the Black race is becoming extinct, Josh explains.

I don't have a hair preference says Josh. I don't really care how a woman wears her hair, he explains. What I care most about is a pretty face and pretty feet, Josh explains. Body size is also not that big of an issue for him. He states that although he has nothing against fat women, he would never date them. I just need honesty and loyalty from a woman, says Josh.

The advice Josh gives to Black women is to be more patient and be confident in themselves.

Comfort Level

When it comes to selecting a mate, Jonathan Dickerson, a native of the Midwest region of the United States, knows exactly what he wants or looks for in a woman. Preferably, a woman should be sincere, self-driven, intelligent, goal-oriented and independent. Also, the woman should be hungry for growth rather than being complacent and having one way of seeing and expecting things to be in life, says Dickerson.

While Dickerson's rearing and lifestyle conditioned him to date women outside of his race, he experienced dating African American women for a short period of time on a casual basis. His preferred way of meeting a woman is through referrals or networks of mutual friends with the relationship being organic rather than a forced type situation, says Dickerson.

Being a descendent of African American parents who raised him in an African Methodist Episcopal Church, Dickerson attended a predominantly White private school from the elementary to the high school level. As a young middle school student, Dickerson never imagined dating outside of his race and thought it to be something not natural and uncomfortable for him. As he entered high school with all of the girls being White, his level of comfort around White people developed and, subsequently, he experienced his first serious relationship with a White woman. The relationship lasted for five years.

Dickerson attended college in the Midwest and earned a Bachelor of Science degree. He continued his first serious relationship with a White woman on an on and off basis. During the interim, he dated African American women, White women and women from other races. The relationships were not serious and lasted for a couple of months, says Dickerson.

As a first round draft choice in the National Football League, Dickerson began his second serious relationship with a Mediterranean woman who was raised around African Americans.

Dickerson met this lady at a special event and started a long distance relationship that lasted for two years.

Afterwards, Dickerson began his third serious relationship with a White woman in the Western Region of the U.S. who he met through a mutual friend. They dated for five years and are now married. According to Dickerson (31), his wife (33) who works in the entertainment industry met all his expectations for a woman such as being sincere, self-driven, intelligent, goal-oriented and independent. She also has a nourishing mentality germane for having his future kids.

As a couple, they have not encountered any racial challenges or barriers. They do have concerns for Dickerson considering the behavior of law enforcement towards African American men. According to Dickerson, he tries to convince his wife that he can properly handle himself in traffic stop situations by the police although she fears he might be the next victim.

Moreover, as a couple, all family members and friends equally embraced them and supported their lifestyles. People in the community where they reside have also been supported of their relationship.

Dickerson's perspective is that White women or people in the community typically don't oppose interracial relationships unless they are racist or are members of a hate group. African American women who are not a part of his circle of friends, typically "will let him know they are not feeling it," so to speak. Dickerson is aware that African American women take offense to African American men dating or marrying outside of their race because it appears that the man does not see the African American woman as worthy or good enough especially when the African American man is a successful person.

According to Dickerson, professional athletes in the NFL are targets for women of all races. Some African American men are accustomed to being in environments (parties, clubs, events, etc.) that exposes them to White women disproportionately to women in their race. They may have already become comfortable or conditioned with White women in similar environments or they may develop a comfort level with White women from these types of settings, says Dickerson.

In seeking to date or marry an African American man, African American women should remain confident in themselves and avoid becoming angry about interracial couples. Their angry mentality works against what they are trying to accomplish, says Dickerson.

Dickerson believes some African American men are disturbed by this level of anger and reluctant to be in a relationship with African American women. Thus, African American women should be self-driven for what they want, get rid of the anger and maintain a positive mental attitude in pursuit of their interest. When you have "so much anger ingrained inside of you, it stops your growth emotionally, socially and spiritually," says Dickerson.

Country Boy

Going to parties, clubs and concerts can be an essential activity for many people. When a man desires not to go to these activities with a girlfriend or wife, his lack of interest can become a disaster to the relationship.

Rodney Foster, a country boy, enjoyed gambling and dating women from different ethnic backgrounds but he rejected the activity of going to parties, clubs and concerts with them. In fact, Foster (age 62) was married to an African American woman for 10 years who had two children of her own. He described her as being a very attractive woman with perfect teeth, legs and body. She was a city girl that resembled Vanessa Williams who was raised in the Mid-Atlantic region of the U.S.

Although Foster agreed that he was equally the problem in the marriage, his African American wife was a gold digger and party goer who loved to be in the streets, so to speak; and she saw Foster as a county hick, someone who loved to stay home, shoot guns and go fishing; so they divorced for irreconcilable differences.

While raised in the South, Foster attended high school at a time of segregation. The predominantly White school where he attended was integrated with African American students, which led to civil unrest, fights and riots.

After graduation, Foster attended one year of college. He then pursued a career in the U.S. Air Force as an avionic technician. Foster gained extensive international traveling experience to different countries and formed relationships with women from these countries. On the average, these relationships lasted for one year and a half year, said Foster.

In finding a mate who was equally yoked, Foster met his White girlfriend after retiring and serving 15 years in the military. They have been together for 20 years. Ironically, the relationship started after Foster met the girlfriend's 17 year-old daughter, said Foster.

At the time, the daughter was destitute, frustrated with her father and needed a place to live. Foster allowed the daughter to stay with him and subsequently the mother wanted to know why the daughter was staying with a stranger. The mother, a retired manager from a food chain and protector of her daughter, became interested in him for providing a home for her daughter. Subsequently, this led to their becoming a couple, said Foster.

As expected, Foster was not initially accepted by the girlfriend's parents who lived in an all White community. The father was one of the "good old boys" so to speak. The mother was quite disrespectful to him, said Foster. Once the father got to know Foster and the mother-in-law became acclimated to his standards during the time that she stayed with the couple, Foster was finally welcomed in the family, said Foster.

While driving Black and with a White woman in the car, Foster gained a negative experience with law enforcement. While in the state of Texas, Foster was traveling on an interstate in the opposite direction of the police. When the police noticed that Foster was a Black man with a White woman in the car, he was "pulled over" by the police.

According to Foster, the police falsely stated that he was stopped for having a damaged tail light. The police further requested that his girlfriend step out of the car and then questioned if she knew Foster. Once she said yes, the police allowed the girlfriend to reenter the car and did not write a ticket for the alleged reason being stopped, said Foster.

As horrible as this incident appears, Foster noted that it did not hamper their relationship. In fact, Foster noted that it strengthen their bond together. The incident also helped the couple to openly discuss current incidents of police brutality although the girlfriend did not understand the meaning of "Black Lives Matter." She would say to him, "I understand your opinion about "Black Lives Matter" but "this is what I see" about the movement, said Foster.

As a context for her thinking, the girlfriend (age 55) was raised in an all White community, attended a parochial school and obviously never "walked in the shoes" of an African American, said Foster.

Despite the challenges of discrimination or race relations in America, Foster is very satisfied with his White girlfriend. According to Foster, he would do anything such as "bust his butt" for her because she totally cares about him and is sensitive to his needs. She, for example, cuts his finger nails, pick the dead skin off of his feet and makes breakfast and lunch for him; whereas, his former African American wife and other African American women did not do those things for him, said Foster.

For an African American woman or any woman seeking to date or marry an African American man, Foster noted that the African American woman should be who she is and allow the man to be who he is. In doing so, you can see who the person is and decide if you want to be with him, said Foster. In essence, don't expect the man to be the type of man you want him to be. Allow him to be himself and not someone else. If you don't like the man, then don't marry him, said Foster.

From experience, Foster emphasized that African American women want a sophisticated man. They don't want a country boy, country hick or farmer type. They frown upon these types of men. So I just walked away from African American women including my former wife. Since I was a gambler and won a lot of money, she only wanted me for the money not the relationship, said Foster.

Curiousity

Oliver Johnston is a 38 year-old African American man; he's single and never been married. Both of Oliver's parents are African American. His father is deceased; and his mother is dating but is not married. Oliver does not identify with any religion; he considers himself a free spirit. Oliver is dating Tammy a 40 year-old White woman. They are both from a city in Texas. Oliver works in a factory that refurbishes computers, and Tammy works in customer service.

Oliver has three children from a previous relationship, and Tammy has two children as well from a previous relationship. The two have no children together.

Oliver met Tammy at a social event. He admitted that he'd always been curious about White women, but the chance had never presented itself until that particular night. Oliver explained that he wasn't sure how to approach her, or how to start the conversation; however, to his delight once the conversation began, they had a lot in common.

How could I not love Black women, said Oliver; or, even be led away from them, Oliver retorted. My Mama is Black, and to turn completely away from Black women, would be like turning from my Mama, explained Oliver. Oliver continued to explain that no factors associated with Black women could turn him completely off from them. Oliver's current relationship is his choice because Tammy is fun and different from other women he dated.

Oliver stated that he's not particularly attracted to a certain type. I like what I like, he said. Whatever shape, size, skin tone, or hair texture attracts me at that time is, what I go for, he said. Oliver explains that he's not particular about specific physical attributes, and doesn't have any reservations about Black women. Of course, there are things about people that bother me, but it's not just about Black women. Women that have some political knowledge, and that aren't easily persuaded by what's fed to us in the news are attractive to me, said Oliver.

Oliver particularly explained that he was curious about White women, and was somewhat apprehensive to date them because of what family might think. He stated that his attitude is generally pro-Black. I support Black people, Black relationships, Black women in general, and I never want to contradict that, he said. He explained that his intentions weren't to seek a White woman, but the relationship sort of "snuck up" on him, he said.

Oliver doesn't really think women should pursue a man; he believes that's the job of the man is to pursue the woman. He also believes friendship is the key to maintaining a positive relationship. Be friends first and get to know the person. This, he believes, creates long-term healthy relationships.

One of the main challenges that I've faced in this relationship is criticism from family, said Oliver. Oliver talked about his family not really accepting Tammy, and even using racial slurs around her. This has pushed him away from some people, which he doesn't enjoy. And, in some cases, it's even made him reevaluate his relationship.

As an advice to African American women, they just have to learn to be patient with their men and learn to listen, said Oliver.

Fitness Matters

Brian Bailey is a married 46 year-old African American man; he was born in a city in Texas, raised in Oklahoma and currently resides in Texas. His parents are both African American, and were married for 50 years. Brian is a Baptist Christian. His wife Ariel is a 45 year-old Hispanic woman. They have two children together. Brian works as a territory manager for a large security company and is an entrepreneurial. Ariel is a sales manager at a local department store. They both have some college experience.

Brian and Ariel met at a networking event. Brian said he felt an immediate attraction and interest in Ariel the first time they met and conversed. During the event, the two exchanged business cards and eventually began to date. Before meeting Ariel, Brian said he dated Black women, and he wasn't sure what made him stop or led him away from Black women. I just knew I wanted Ariel, said

Brian. As in any relationship, he said, we've had our challenges, but I learned a lot from her along the way.

As far as hair, I do love the simplicity of my wife's hair, said Brian. He and his wife are avid fitness people, so the worry about hair is never an excuse or a reason for her to not want to workout. Being fit and keeping in shape are a passion of Brian's, and he expects his woman to share that same passion. This, he explains, was not a quality he found in many Black women.

Brian said the easiest way for a woman to pursue him would be through fitness and training. Brian also explained that there weren't many distinct differences in his marriage in comparison to his previous relationships with Black women. Culturally speaking, Hispanic women are similar to Black women in many ways especially concerning health and fitness, he explained. However, he elaborated on the point that he and his wife both enjoy staying fit, and they make an effort together to keep their bodies in shape. This, he explained, isn't always the case with other Hispanic women. For instance, Brian talked about family members of Ariel's that have chosen to indulge in unhealthy eating habits and as a result are obese.

Brian talked about his experiences with Black women that questioned his reason for stepping outside of his race; he explained that people should be able to date or marry whomever they choose. Race, in his opinion, shouldn't be a deciding factor. What matters is the type of woman she is, explained Brian. I am attracted and sought women, for instance, that were health conscious, smart and attractive, he said.

In relationships, Brian suggests that women show their true selves before committing to a long-term relationship. He uses the example concerning fitness, and explained how a woman will pretend to be interested in fitness, just to get involved, but eventually reveals a dislike once in the relationship. This creates, in his opinion, tension and makes the relationship harder for both people.

Foreign Interest

Vincent Henderson is a 32 year-old single African man; he was married to an African American woman for five years. Vincent was born in England. His current girlfriend, Isabella, is a Mexican American. Vincent's parents are both African, and currently live in Nigeria. They have been married for 37 years. Vincent associates himself as a Christian. He has no children and neither does his girlfriend Isabella. Isabella was born in Mexico, but attended high school in Texas. She has some college, but didn't graduate. Vincent has a bachelor's degree in Management Information Systems and a second bachelor's degree in Finance.

Vincent and Isabella met at the gym. Vincent married an older African American woman when he was just finishing college. That experience left a bad impression on him about African American women. However, it didn't fully deter him from dating Black women. I never stopped dating Black women, and I don't know that I'm done dating them, says Vincent. My last situation didn't work out, that's all, says Vincent. I just wasn't in love with my ex-wife, explains Vincent. She had a bad temper. She had three kids, and one was very close to my age. It was a weird situation. I kind of went into it with an open heart, but it turned out to be chaotic, says Vincent.

Vincent explains that his attraction has no color or race boundaries. I'm not particularly just attracted to only Black women. It's the aura, or just how I feel about and around them, says Vincent. I think with Black women, it's more so their attitude that kind of turns me on, Vincent explains. I'm attracted to strength in Black women. Their ability to hold their own, says Vincent.

Vincent isn't particular about hair, as long as they aren't bald, he says. He also doesn't have any particular preference about skin color; he's open to all shades. I don't care about color, light skin, purple skin; it doesn't matter to me, says Vincent.

Body size isn't a deal breaker for Vincent either. It doesn't matter what size she is, as long as it's not just colossal, he says. If someone is thick and big, and they got curves or whatever, I'm cool with that, as long as she doesn't have to shop for clothes at Rooms To Go, we're good, he says.

Vincent talks passionately about his reservations about Black women. Anger turns me off. A lot of African American women are very bitter. He said, actually most of them are very bitter. A man has to do a whole lot of convincing. Black women have too many defenses, walls, and defense mechanisms, said Vincent. But, if you really think about it, you can't blame them, he said.

Vincent explains no particular factors led him to date outside of his race. I was just attracted to my Mexican girlfriend's spirit, says Vincent. I also went through a phase where I just wanted to be with a woman that spoke a different language. I've dated a French woman and a Russian woman, just to hear them speak something different than English, says Vincent.

Vincent is not about the games when being approached. He expects women to pursue him with honest intentions. There's no certain way, but if we decide to do something, let's not play games, says Vincent. I don't want to play that "tit for tat." Just be real, and at least give me the benefit of the doubt, says Vincent.

The difference Vincent notices with Mexican women in comparison to Black women are their less dramatic ways, but this also bores him. It's kind of like, if I say jump, she jumps. I'll ask her something, but she has no authentic voice. It's always about what I like. Black women have a voice, but sometimes the voice is projected to be on a megaphone, exclaims Vincent.

A few ways Vincent has learned to keep his relationship positive is to have an open mind, and be respectful of the differences. The whole adaptation thing is a major barrier because it takes some time to get use to the differences, says Vincent. After dating a Black person for so many years and then moving to a different culture, it can be hard. Mexicans do a lot of kissing each other in the mouth. I don't understand that. It's just different; they're too touchy and affectionate, says Vincent. Going out in public has some barriers; we catch looks a lot. I can see people wonder, what's their story. I see it on their faces, explains, Vincent. Communication skills, honesty, and constructive criticism are important to me, says Vincent. I don't like people that only want to talk about the bad.

The advice Vincent would give an African American woman, he says, it's kind of a slippery slope. I just think Black women have taken this independent thing, and turned it into a cop-out, to not fulfill their matrimonial and parenting duties. Everybody has rules in life, and I don't mean that you're to be somebody's door mat, but there is a certain level of submissiveness that's allowed and necessary. The whole new independent thing has been taken to a whole different level. Be submissive, says Vincent.

Fraternity Life

Gordon Duncan, a native of New York, is a 22-year old college student in Georgia who not only became a member of a White fraternity but also president of the fraternity. Since Black fraternities at the college did not allow students to attend a rush their freshman year, Duncan was encouraged by his White best friend and roommate to attend a rush along with him at several White fraternities. This experience led to Duncan and his friend pledging eight and a half weeks as freshmen and subsequently becoming a fraternity brother.

Duncan was popular at the college particularly among his fraternity brothers as he became president of the fraternity his junior year. In the same year, Duncan met his girlfriend, currently a 21-year old Asian American. She approached him at the college's homecoming football game and gave him her telephone number for a possible date. At the time, Duncan was preoccupied as he was watching his homecoming date, a biracial cheerleader participate in the homecoming festivities. After the football game, he took the cheerleader to a party and dinner the same night. He described her as being very attractive, light complexion and having curly light hair.

Prior to Duncan connecting with his current girlfriend and dating her for two years, he dated another girl that was bi-racial for approximately one year and a half. This experience was in high school and a few months in college. Although many African American men experience racism in numerous ways, Duncan indicated that he has never experienced racism in life. For example, he has never experienced racism among members in his White fraternity and individuals on the college campus. He has never experienced racism or backlash while driving, walking or holding hands with his girlfriend in public, says Duncan.

While his girlfriend's parents and siblings welcomed him to the family, Duncan cited one incident of her older brother using a racial comment towards him. Duncan said, the girlfriend's brother was upset with her while under the influence of alcohol. The brother sent a negative text to the girlfriend calling Duncan an ignorant negro. The next day, the brother realized he was wrong and apologized to both of them via text.

Having attended predominantly White public schools and formed friendship with mostly White males, Duncan looks for certain traits in a woman whom he decides to date. He said, "the woman has to be driven and independent, possesses a sense of humor, is highly intelligent and a good communicator and knows what makes him and her upset." In establishing a relationship with his Asian girlfriend, Duncan says she met all of these qualities. He was very impressed with her working two jobs while attending college full-time. Although she initially approached him, he was also attracted to her looks. Duncan described his girlfriend as having a beautiful body shape (5'7, 140 pounds), strong athletic legs, olive skin, brown eyes, long black hair and very pretty and attractive.

Duncan said, he does not have a problem with a woman wearing weaves or putting on make-up, but his preference is to be with a woman who displays the natural beauty as in his current and past girlfriend.

While close to graduating from college, Duncan is wondering about his future with his girlfriend in mind. He mentioned having "cold feet" or having to break up with her for four days in order to assess whether she is the person he should marry and have children with her. Duncan explained that being in a relationship for approximately two years is enough time for him to determine if his girlfriend is the right person for him.

The advice that Duncan gives to an African American woman seeking to date or marry an African American man is to continue to work on yourself and be who you are. Personally, he prefers a woman who is transparent and willing to let him know openly that she is interested in him. At the same time, he prefers the woman to be driven, hard working and independent, says Duncan.

Life's Perspective

Carlton Sims is a 36 year-old man from a city in Georgia. Both of Carlton's parents are African American, and have been married for almost 60 years. Carlton was raised in the Catholic Church. He's dating Christian, a 26 year-old Brazilian-American woman. Neither of them have children. Carlton graduated from a historically Black college earning a bachelor and master's degree. Currently, he owns a graphic design company. Christian attended college and is a model. They both reside in a city in Florida.

Carlton met Christian at a social mixer on South Beach in Florida. Carlton explained that he's dated a variety of different women throughout his adult life. I'm from the Atlanta area, so most of my early dating experiences were with Black women, he said. Having graduated from a Black college, he also talked about having several relationships and experiences with Black women on campus.

Two main factors that led me to date different races were my moving to South Florida and starting my own business, he explained. I interact with all different types, cultures, and races of people on a daily basis. There's no shortage of beautiful women in South Florida, and I'm attracted to beautiful women that are ambitious and grounded, said Carlton.

Carlton also talked about the importance of women keeping their bodies in good physical shape. In addition to being an entrepreneur, he also works as a personal trainer and prefers a woman that is physically appealing to him. He explained she doesn't have to work out as often as he does, but he's attracted to women that keep fit. Carlton explained that he has no prejudices against hair or complexion. I like a woman that feels good about herself. However, the way she chooses to wear her hair is up to her, he said. As long as she's put together and smells good, then I'm cool with it, he explained.

Carlton said, I enjoy being with my girl; she makes me laugh. We have fun, he explained. I think that's what makes it work, Carlton expressed. Carlton talked about how the differences in age and culture play a small part in their relationship. He talked about some moments that he might have to elaborate on certain subjects that he wouldn't have to with a Black woman, or maybe a woman closer to 40. I'm a pretty patient type of guy, said Carlton. I think that plays a role in the relationship too, Carlton explained.

I don't really see any barriers or challenges at this point in my relationship. It's somewhat a new thing, and I don't put too much thought into the problems. I operate from a day-to-day basis. I don't know that this is a forever thing, but it's a good time for now, said Carlton. Carlton said the qualities that he looks for in a woman are loyalty and her perspective about life. I like to know what a person's outlook on life is, he said. Is she grounded, patient, and supportive? Can she cook? or Is she willing to learn how to cook? This is an important quality for Carlton as well.

The advice he offers to Black women is to not get wrapped up in temporary feelings because whatever it is, is probably just a feeling of the moment. Think before you put certain "words out there in the streets" about your man. Be patient and enjoy the person you chose to be with, he said.

Limited Supply

When there is a limited supply of goods, the price for that product is typically higher. When there is a high supply of goods, the price for that product is typically lower. With regard to a relationship, Peter Knight recognizes that there are a limited number of African American men available for African American women to date or marry. His rationale is that society has intentionally destroyed our leaders such as Martin Luther King Jr. and implemented laws regarding drug use that disproportionally affects African American men; and, subsequently, lowers the chances of African American women marrying an African American man.

While raised on the east coast by two parents, Knight (age 42) dated a number of African American women of different complexions (dark and light skinned). With two influential men in his life being a "player" of women (father and cousin), Knight adopted their behavior and became non-committed to most women with whom he formed relationships.

Having a childhood crush on his stepmother (African American) who was "high yellow or light complexion," Knight became attracted to a woman of similar features. He fell in love with an African American woman of similar characteristics and dated her for one year.

Although Knight had circled White girls in his middle school year book who he saw was attractive to him, it was not until Knight was a senior in high school that he dated a White woman. The young lady was always around him and subsequently he loss his virginity to her on his 17th Birthday. Unbeknownst to him, the woman became pregnant; she had an abortion due to her parents not wanting her to have a child from an African American man. Subsequently, they ended the relationship after several months together.

Later in life, Knight fell in love again when he dated a light complexioned woman for three years who had a White mother and an African American father. Having the complexion of his preference, Knight indicated the relationship became very serious where they moved in together but the relationship ended when the girlfriend was incarcerated for criminal acts such as thief.

In the late 1980's, Knight met his White wife (Betsy) through a customer at a store where he worked. Betsy was a high school dropout and from a poor, racist (trailer park type family) with no interest in education. The customer, an African American man, was in a relationship with Betsy's best friend who was Asian. In order to have more quality time with his girlfriend and have a couple to mingle with occasionally, the customer told Knight that he had a friend who he thought would be a good mate for him. When Knight met the customer's friend who had a child from another relationship, they talked extensively and became friends.

Betsy relocated to another city and became pregnant by Knight; they moved in together as a couple three years later. When Betsy became pregnant again, they married and took on the responsibility of raising all three children. Having ideas for a quality life, Knight encouraged Betsy to go back to school to complete her high school diploma and graduate from college. This led to Betsy earning a good paying job.

Knight, a blue-collar worker with a high school diploma, has been married to his wife (age 39) for 15 years and has encountered numerous challenges as a married couple. One example included his wife being disrespected and denied privileges on the job due to her being married to an African American man. The unfair treatment forced Betsy to quit her job. Another challenge included their daughter being discriminated against at a preschool day care where the teachers reluctantly refused to accept her race as African American. Instead, they would acknowledge her as a White person since she was of very light complexion with Caucasian features. When Knight went to the day care, the teachers' attitudes changed. "I am the reason my daughter is African American," said Knight.

Furthermore, Knight experienced racial tension from his wife's parents and derogatory remarks from his cousin. Being a "player" of women, the cousin could not understand how Knight could fall for a woman and one particularly a White woman. He would constantly belittle Knight about his decision realizing there were many women who were chasing Knight.

Betsy's parents and especially the grandfather, maintained their bias and stereotypes of African American men as drug dealers. They saw Knight as one of them. It was not until Knight loss his temper with the grandfather and apologized for wrongdoing that they put away their differences and enjoyed each other's company.

With the ongoing occurrence of police brutality, Knight indicated that he has periodic discussions with his wife and children about the matter. Betsy is very disturbed about the unfair treatment of African American men and afraid that Knight could be a victim of such circumstance. The children are oblivious to the matter. They have friends from different races who they communicate with on a daily basis, said Knight.

While many African American women have a difficult time of dating and marrying an African American man, Knight notes several reasons for this problem. First, Knight indicates that there are a limited number of African American men available to date or marry African American women as result of society's goal to destroy them. "I look at the male cousins in my immediate family (ages 21, 24, 30, 36 and 38) and find that most of them are immature, indecisive, uneducated and victimized by the criminal system," said Knight. Second, Knight feels that African American women are too selective or particular in choosing an African American man and this subsequently leaves them being without a man. Third, they set their standards too high and undermine the value of a man who is a blue-collar worker such as a UPS employee. They also look for the same type of African American man and can't be happy. They have high expectation; whereas the White woman has no expectation, says Knight.

With this in mind, Knight feels it is best for the African American woman to find a friend or someone who is ready to be with her. You can't force yourself into a relationship, says Knight.

Love Oneself

Vincent Loving is a 36 year-old African American man. He was born in a city in Florida, and currently lives in Florida. His parents are both African American and have been married for over 41 years. Vincent was raised a Baptist Christian, and is currently still a Christian. His girlfriend Brea is a White 33 year-old woman. Vincent has one son from a previous relationship, but has none with Brea. Brea has no children of her own. Vincent works in healthcare at an elderly home facility. Brea is a nurse and is also from Florida.

Vincent met Brea at work. They became familiar with each other through their working relationship, which then turned into a friendship, and eventually a relationship. She's a genuinely caring person, and he found her to be very attractive, said Vincent.

Vincent has dated several different races including Black women. I like the idea of mixing and mingling with different cultures and races. I think that's what led me away from solely dating Black women, explained Vincent. Vincent elaborated on his attraction to women; he explained that the laws of attraction for him have several layers. I want to be intrigued first. Something about her has to make me wonder, he said.

Vincent explains that time plays a major role in his relationships. He works long hours, and seeks women that are flexible with their time. Vincent explained that these are the things that attract him to women. He likes women of all types, he said. I've dated them all, Black, Hispanic, White, Asian, so I don't discriminate, he said.

Vincent explained that the one reservation he has with Black women is their lack of understanding; so many of the Black women I've encountered are fighting through anger and aggression towards the Black man, especially ones like me, he said. I have no borders or boundaries regarding race, and not all Black women can accept that, Vincent explained.

Vincent further expressed his concern with the Black woman harboring unconscious anger for the Black man, which he believes is one of the reasons so many Black men and women are at odds. Maybe it's the reason, he said, that some Black men choose to date outside their race. Sometimes one needs a break from the fight, I guess, he said. Vincent made it clear that this, however, could never keep him away from Black women; its that he's just open to date whomever he's attracted to as a potential mate.

Vincent likes women that are bold, and if they were to approach him, he'd want them to be bold and secure. I think I've become oblivious to color, he said. If people in society dislike who I date, that's not my problem, Vincent explained. Vincent, however, made it clear that racial injustice is prevalent, and it is present in his relationship. He emphasizes that he personally chooses to disregard it.

The advice that Vincent offers women is to love themselves; he's found that, regardless of race, the women who loved and were confident in themselves, made great partners.

Man Attraction

Once upon a time the women did not know me, now they are all over me, was the background of Ricky Patterson. From elementary to high school, Patterson never had a girlfriend because he weighed over 300 pounds. Once Patterson lost 100 pounds, he could not keep the girl off him, so to speak. He dated several African American women for approximately three to six months before he started his career.

Patterson's career path led him to study marine engineering and earn a BS degree. From his roots of being born in Illinois and taking a year of college courses in the same state, he entered the U.S. Navy to complete his degree and work in the field of marine engineering. Patterson retired after serving his country for 16 years. He currently works in transportation.

While in the Navy, Patterson met his first Japanese girlfriend in Japan. He also met his Filipino wife in the Philippines. They were married for 10 years and have three children together who are college graduates. Patterson described his first wife as being a poor communicator and gambler who stayed away from their home for long periods of time.

After retiring from the military and his Filipino wife leaving him with the three children, Patterson dated a White woman for five years and an African American woman for five years. The relationship with the African American woman became very serious whereby they were engaged and Patterson allowed the woman and her adult children to move in with him.

Because of Patterson's battle with cancer, the death of his mother and stress from his girlfriends' children, the relationship ended disappointingly. The girlfriend was considered his "best friend" and the ideal partner of how he liked to be treated in a relationship. Although they participated in counseling, he could not deal with the abusive and violent behavior of the girlfriend's daughter, says Patterson.

Patterson, age 54, was raised Baptist and is currently married to a White woman for over a year after dating her for seven years. Together they are raising an adopted grandchild of the wife and allowed two of the wife's adult children to move in with them. As a native of Montana, Patterson wife age 55, was raised Methodist and has four adult children from a previous relationship. The wife earned a BS degree in Interior Design and is employed in city government. The couple attends the Methodist church together.

With his African American friend being in the Navy and married to a White woman, Patterson met his current wife at his friend's Thanksgiving dinner. To make sure the relationship was a good match, Patterson said that they started talking as friends and dated for seven years before getting married. Patterson said he was attracted to his wife because she was very classy and talkative. He also needed a friend after disappointingly and reluctantly separating from his African American girlfriend.

When Patterson felt that the relation of his new girlfriend was falling apart, they separated for two months and went through counseling to learn how to listen and communicate with each other and subsequently resolved their differences. Patterson said the main concern was to ensure that his wife, girlfriend at the time, was serious about him and their relations as a married couple.

As a part of challenges in an interracial marriage, sometimes there can be barriers spearheaded by family members and other people in the community. For instance, Patterson indicated that his White wife's family did not initially approve of their being a couple. There was a lot of racial tension. Some family members would call him negro through his wife but not to him in person. His wife's children were at odds as well. Patterson said, however, this was not the case for his family members. They accepted his wife into the family although the children initially wanted him to be happy through traveling, being financially secured and avoid tying himself down to anyone.

Since Patterson and his wife reside in a upscale military community outside of the state of Washington, they are welcomed by other interracial couples and have not experienced barriers as a couple. When the couple initially visited the wife's parents all White community, they experienced racial profiling by the police until Patterson filed a complaint with the community's police department and threatened to report the department to the U.S. Attorney General's office.

While there is no perfect marriage, Patterson advises a Black woman and any other woman to "stop looking for a man and find a friend." He feels it is much easier for you to love a friend than for you to love a man. Ideally, a best friend is a person whom a woman can fall in love with and have a lasting and memorable relationship. The friend is someone a woman can relate and communicate well with on all subject matters. So the key is to get to know the man as a person and be patient in the process, says Patterson.

Although Patterson was engaged to marry an African American woman who was his "best friend," he expressed that the biracial community where he resided contributed to his marrying outside of his race. There were few African American women residing in the community and most of them were married.

Military Love

Paul Bridgewater is an African American man who was born in a small town in Arkansas, and his Hispanic wife was born in a metropolitan city in Texas. They have been married for three years and have one child together. Bridgewater has three other children from two African American women. Bridgewater met his wife of the same age (33) in the U.S. Army Reserve. He was raised a Baptist by a single parent, and his wife was raised Catholic by two parents. Bridgewater earned a Bachelor of Science in Finance and works in the Army Reserve as a data analyst. His wife earned an Associate of Arts in General Studies and works in the Army Reserve as a HR clerk.

Realizing he was tired of playing the field with African American women, Bridgewater says there was really no difference in dating in or outside of his race except for skin color. The attitudes of the

African American women who he dated were the same as the attitudes of his wife. However, he prefers a woman that is cute, intelligent, and independent. He also prefers a woman who can communicate well with him, works well with his children, and has career goals. Bridgewater says marrying a Hispanic woman was predicated on his being mature at the time and focused on his career rather than any negative traits or attributes of an African American woman. Bridgewater says he simply "messed up with the African American women" because of his behavior.

Bridgewater commends his Hispanic wife for encouraging him to focus on his career and completing a BS in Finance since he did not get the same level of motivation from the African American mothers of his three children. He felt the relationships with the African American girlfriends were unhealthy, in a gridlock or stuck in the sand, so to speak. He expressed that this problem was heightened by unnecessary confrontation from one of the girlfriends and her family members. Bridgewater said that this girlfriend was not ambitious and took a job just to have one although she had a college degree. He also explained that she became resentful that she did not get the same benefits of his wife such as marriage and a house. Subsequently, this led to a custody dispute over the child they had together.

While being in an interracial marriage, Bridgewater faced challenges from his Hispanic wife's family. Since her family members did not speak English, some family members resented Bridgewater dating outside of his race. This was not a part of the Hispanic culture, says Bridgewater. The family men in his wife's family told him, "You need to go and date your own race." Over a period of time, other family members along with his wife eased the tension and helped everyone understand that they have a right to marry and be with whomever they chose.

Although Bridgewater and his wife lived in a community where interracial marriage was the norm, he noted that outside of the community they faced people who opposed interracial marriage. One example included a coworker of Bridgewater's wife who did not agree with African American men dating outside of their race. Another example included Bridgewater's wife being questioned by strangers as to "what she was doing with African American children."

Considering African American women are having a difficult time dating and marrying African American men, Bridgewater advises that African American women should "have and maintain a positive attitude in a relationship, believe in their man, don't jump to conclusions about things, put your man down or give up on him and be willing to listen to the man before you react on something." Bridgewater says this advice applies to the man as well.

Mother's Influence

The most influential person in the world is a mother. When choosing a girlfriend or wife, many males choose a person with similar attributes as their mother. Ricky Martin, for instance, became interested and committed to his girlfriend because she resembled attributes of his mother. Martin said his girl friend is a Christian, smart, mentally tough, hard working and a problem bearer. She is a good counselor to her family members and strong enough to carry his burden when he needs it.

Martin, age 25, was born in the Midwest where he attended a predominantly African American school. He was a stellar football athlete in high school earning him a full football scholarship at a small predominantly white college in Illinois. Martin's All American status, along with his outgoing personality and good rapport with people, made him a popular person on the college campus. He dated women of different races such as White, Hispanic, and Asian, as well as two African American women in high school and college. Most of the relationships lasted for only a few months.

Martin said, "I was very interested in the last African American woman I dated before meeting my current girlfriend. She checked out for me, so to speak. I thought she was going to be my future girlfriend. But the timing was not right and she was not mature enough for us to sustain a relationship. She was trying to determine who she was and whether or not she believed in God. She was trying to determine the things she wanted to do in life. This was a deterrent to me. I could not see myself being in a long-term relationship with a person and having children with someone who did not believe in God and did not know what she wanted to do in life. On one day, the conversation was about her wanting to have children by the time she was 28. On another day, the conversation was about her having difficulties in figuring out what she wanted to be in life. Where she was in the period of her life did not allow for growth. My preference is to be in a relationship with someone who loves the Lord and is mature," said Martin.

While a senior in college, Martin met the lady of his life at an overnight mission trip affiliated with the college. The students participated in a service-learning project. Martin was initially impressed with his girlfriend placing her hair in a ponytail and doing the dirty work the guys normally would do. He described her as being a very attractive and smart White girl who loves the Lord. When Martin approached his girlfriend (currently age 24), he did not think she would want to date him. The words he heard on the campus were that she did not date anybody and overlooked everybody who approached her. She was an honor roll student who focused on her academics while maintaining a 4.0 grade point average.

Surprisingly, she gave him her telephone number and they started dating and building on the relationship for three years. After graduating from college and living in different cities, they recently decided to move in together in a city where Martin resides. According to Martin, they are getting married in the near future.

In any relationship, there are going to be some trials and tribulations. Martin was fully warned by his mother that people are not going to like his being in a relationship with a White woman and that he was going to have to be okay with their perspective and deal with the situation.

As knowledgeable as mothers' normally are, Martin faced opposition to being in a relation with a White woman from his family, friends and his girlfriend's family. According to Martin, his girlfriend's parents said they were just sad that she ended up dating a Black guy. A friend of Martin's mother said she just did not like to see a Black man dating a White woman.

Martin indicated that knowing some people disapprove of your values is one thing but hearing them say that they disapprove your values is another. In fact, Martin said that hearing this was a hurtful thing to him and his girlfriend. They could not understand why family members and others felt this way. They initially struggled with this.

For better understanding of the situation, Martin said that his mother indicated to him "as a parent, you have expectations of how you want your children's life to be. When you see the expectations are not being met, it shakes you up a little bit. It is not a matter of disapproval of your children's decision, but you have to reshape your focus." Additionally, Martin recalled his mother saying, "How can I continue to love and support my children? Dating or marrying someone from another race was not my expectation and nor your girlfriend parents' expectation. So you have to deal with the situation and make the best of it."

There is a beauty in an interracial relationship, but many people that grew up before his era have a different experience and connotation about it, said Martin. While racism and discrimination are rampant in our communities, Martin recognized that he does not know and understand everything about the White culture and his girlfriend does not know and understand everything about the African American culture. But they have intense conversations about race relations such as "Black Lives Matter" and other matters confronting the African American community. You have to live in the skin of certain races in order to fully understand the culture, said Martin.

For African American women seeking to date or marry an African American man, Martin encourages every person to make it about your values rather than your race. My girlfriend could have been Mexican or Asian, but where my values are and where her values are allowed for the relationship to work out. In my opinion, it is more than my being attracted to an African American woman or White woman. It is all about understanding my values and making sure my values align with the person I am in a relationship with. It is all about someone who accepts my values, treats me well and is going to be with me for a long time. Thus, I am so proud of who I chose to be my mate. If I die, I feel she can carry the load with or without me, said Martin.

My Angel

God moves in mysterious ways are the testimonies of many people especially when they survive a tragedy or overcome a major situation in life. Phillip Grant, a 60 year-old African American man who was born in the Midwest and resides in the Southwest, is a witness to God's blessings. While dealing with an alcohol addiction issue, Grant lost his driver's license to the judicial system on the charges of driving while intoxicated (DWI).

Carrying the burden of not being able to legally drive his car and having to work through the judicial system to regain his license,

Grant was in a situation he had never experienced in his entire life. Grant needed something in his life to help him work through the dilemma. Not looking for a relationship, Grant met Penny Flores, a 45 year-old Mexican woman through a mutual friend. The friend dated Flores' sister and worked at the same company as Grant and Flores. Flores has two children (19 and 22); and she works in the cleaning department at the company. Grant has no children, and he works in the security department at the company.

According to Grant, Flores is "my angel." She is my spirit. She embraces me as I am. We have grown to enjoy being around each other for the eight months that we have been together. We started the relationship talking as friends before getting sexually involved with each other. Currently, I am just taking one day at a time with Flores and not jumping the gun, so to speak, says Grant.

In the past, Grant had dated women of various races such as Hispanic, Asian, Filipino, Korean, White and African American when he was in the military. After the military, he primarily dated African American women on an on-and-off basis. I had women in different cities and states and was never really serious about any of them. I was out of control; chasing women was like an addiction, says Grant.

Flores came into my life at a time when I am not young as I used to be; I had been in the game chasing women long enough and life was getting boring, says Grant. At this time, I really enjoy being with Flores. Our dating feels like high school dating all over again, says Grant. On my 60th birthday, Flores overwhelmed me with nice gifts that really touched me. This was combined with a dinner date with my friend and his companion. On her 45th birthday, I reciprocated my affection for Flores and showered her with nice gifts too, says Grant.

As a couple, we have not experienced any racism or racial remarks from people in the community. We have, however, witnessed stares from Mexicans and African Americans. To my satisfaction, Flores is like an African American woman. She works hard and takes care of her children. She is also old-fashioned, enjoys cooking meals for me and brings me food on the job, says Grant.

The advice I give to an African American woman who is seeking to date or marry an African American man and maintain a positive relationship is to get to know the man and determine if he is the right person for you. Don't immediately jump in bed with him. Try to enjoy each other first through an activity such as a movie. Take it slow. This is what I am currently doing with Flores, says Grant. Ideally, you want to be happy in your relationship. So don't waste your time being with someone who can't make you happy, says Grant.

No Animosity

Donte Staples is a single 36-year old African American man. He's never been married. Both of his parents are African Americans and are divorced. He is from Illinois. Neither of his parents re-married. Donte said he considers himself to be of a spiritual nature, rather than religious. He also isn't affiliated with a church. Donte has no children, but his girlfriend Maria, a White woman from Illinois, has one son.

Donte is a graduate of a historically Black college. He currently works as a Global Ambassador at a museum in Illinois. Maria and Donte met through mutual friends. He has throughout his life dated and continues to date African American women. Donte said there's something powerful about being in a relationship with an African American woman; however, dating White women gives him a break from tension, anger and animosity that are characteristics of the African American woman. He explains that with a White woman there's this absence of emotional and societal abuse present in the relationship. There's no covert or suppressed animosity or tensions to overcome with a White woman, he explained.

Donte doesn't believe there are factors that have led him away from African American women; he, however, stated that in his last relationship, there was a lack of spontaneity and authenticity. He explained spontaneity and the state of being present don't necessarily have to do with race, but he's noticed that White women often times are able to be present with greater ease than African American women. When his previous African American girl friend were together, for example, they argued more about why they did not spend time together instead of just being together. This was bothersome and pushed him away, said Donte.

Donte has no one specific preference about hair, body size, or complexion. He said that he loves a feminine woman; one who takes good care of herself, has soft skin and smells like a woman. Femininity is important, said Donte. She must carry herself like a woman, he said. In dating African American and White women, Donte said there weren't any differences that he could elaborate on, other than the obvious cultural differences. He said that regardless of race, his place as an African American man always remains. Donte admits that his experiences with African American women gives him a sense of pride, that he misses while in his current relationship.

Donte had no societal pressures or racially charged experiences with his current girlfriend; he expressed that most people are understanding or conditioned to see relationships like his, so it's no big deal, he said. Donte said a challenge he's noticed about African American women is their inability to be realistic about today's over-sexualized society. African American women are too easily disturbed by men's visual stimulation or unattached and distant attention to other women, he explained. Everywhere you look, especially on social media outlets, there's some type of attractive or appealing woman.

African American women have to learn to be secure in themselves and trusting of their man. This is something I've found to not be as big of an issue for White women, Donte said. Donte said he seeks and is attracted to women that know how to be a woman and can "balance him" or do things he can't do. A woman must know how to be a nurturer and can take care of home, Donte explained. He also expressed that he looks for women that are able to code switch, insofar as, she's able to act appropriately according to the setting. He explained that this characteristic has nothing to do with race, but is the type of woman he's attracted to.

Donte's advice to African American women is to be a shoulder for your man and to create a space at home that is of peace and not stressful.

Not Black Enough

Cameron Richie experienced mistreatment by other students as a middle and high school student. While living in the South, Cameron attended a pre-dominantly African American school. He had no problem interacting with his African American peers, and they accepted him as a part of them including the African American girls he dated. When Cameron moved to Virginia and attended a predominantly White school, his life changed. The few African American girls at the school who Cameron sought to date declined to give him the time of day, said Cameron. They saw Cameron as "not being Black enough" because he did not talk, act and dress like the few African American guys and girls at the school.

This devastated Cameron for many years, and he did not feel good about himself. Cameron said this situation led him to date girls outside of his race with low self-esteem and confidence in themselves. In the 11th grade, Cameron began adapting the culture of the African Americans at the school in order to fit in with his race and date African American girls. Cameron said he had to reinvent himself or give up everything he liked doing to be accepted among the Black students at the school. The Black girls said I was a White boy type, so I had to change or be left without a date from a Black girl, said Cameron. When he first attempted to change, a Black boy at a party shouted, "look who is being Black today."

Cameron is 32 years-old and was raised by two African American parents who have been married for over 35 years. As a child, Cameron worshiped in a Baptist church. Currently, he is engaged to Karen, a White woman who is 35 years old. They have one child together. Collectively, they are raising five children. Two of Cameron's children are from a previous relationship with a White woman. Karen's two children are from a previous relationship she had with another man.

At age 27, Cameron met Karen through a mutual friend at a restaurant. She came into his life at a critical time when he emphatically needed someone who could support his social and emotional needs. Cameron was still mentally disturbed by his school experience of having to change his entire identity in order to belong. Cameron said Karen is very supportive and understanding. From a longevity standpoint, she is someone who can take care of him, and he plans to marry her in 2018. Karen is a college graduate and works in the healthcare field as a nurse. Cameron works in real estate and medical supplies.

As a couple, Cameron said they have not faced any racial challenges from people in the community other than some older White people staring and making sarcastic comments to Karen. Cameron also noted that Karen parents gracefully accepted him into their family. With Karen's father being a History teacher and teaching his children about the legacy of African Americans, this made it easy for Cameron to be embraced by the family. In fact, Cameron said he has learned so much about African American history through Karen because of her father. This contributes to the couple having positive discussions about social injustices regarding Black people in the U.S., said Cameron.

Cameron made it perfectly clear that he enjoyed dating African American women. Although he was instantly attracted to Karen, he said that she could have being an African American woman. Karen was new to the community and we started talking and enjoyed each other's conversation, said Cameron.

In responding to the questions about his advice on African American women seeking to date or marry an African American man, Cameron said, "don't be afraid to try different things such as bungee jumping; be open-minded; and enjoy life."

No Depth

Joshua Hinton is a single 34 year-old African American man. He was born in a city in Texas and currently resides in Texas. Joshua has never been married. Both of his parents are African Americans; they were married but are now both deceased. His girlfriend, Layla, is a 30 year-old White woman. She was born in a city in Texas and works in higher education. Joshua has multiple degrees and is currently a medical doctor. He has no children and neither does Layla.

Joshua and Layla met through mutual friends. He explained that the reason he was led away from dating African American women was the lack of depth he experienced in his previous relationship. He needed a change, he said. He hadn't reached a level of comfort that inspired him to take the relationships to the next level with African American women, and particularly in his last relationship. There were so many things such as personality and commonality that stood in the way of the relationship, he said. This made it hard for him to move forward and is what essentially pushed him towards change.

As for the laws of attraction, Joshua is a believer that what you put out, is what comes back to you. This is true in relationships as well, he explained. For this reason, he said, he tries to maintain an overall positive disposition. He explained that a positive nature is what guides his interest and what he considers compatible characteristic. In my older age, I'm attracted to open-mindeness and the ability to grow with a person, said Joshua. The patterns of conversations are important to me as well, he said. I like a sense of humor, someone that's personable, and that can stimulate my mind, explained Joshua. I'm not too concerned about body size, but I do like curvy women, and I prefer natural hair. I'm not particular about skin tone, he said. Joshua explains that one of the issues with African American women is their insecurities and authenticity after they find out that he's a doctor.

In general, I think a lot of sisters are intimidated not by me, but by what I represent. I think it causes them to have insecurities about what they bring to the table, said Joshua. Joshua also discussed his concern with some women being attracted to the things that are associated with him and his accomplishments. He said that most African American women perceive him as a hot commodity among other African American men. Joshua states that there's something very attractive about an aggressive balance. He elaborated on the good feeling of a woman taking time to find out his likes and dislikes, and uses that information to pique his interest. However, he explains that there's a fine line between this type of attention. He isn't interested in women who pursue too strong, but prefers a woman who is somewhat subtle. Joshua said that there are obvious differences that stand out to him, which include not being as aggressive or boisterous. From his experience, White women tend to be more submissive too. They don't ask for much, just company, said Joshua. He realizes that trust needs to be established first in a relationship. There must be common goals and common interests; personal objectives, personal and professional goals need to be aligned, said Joshua. These qualities are essential components to maintaining a positive relationship.

Joshua elaborated on societal pressures of his interracial dating, and explained that our current social climate for Black and White affairs plays a major impactful role in his relationship. He is concerned often that there may not be a genuine acceptance of him among her family. Also, cultural differences are often misunderstood. Layla may not always understand or even be able to empathize with the concern he has as an African American man each day he leaves the house. His frustrations with society can sometimes be misconstrued, which often times puts some strain on his relationship. Nevertheless, Joshua said that he seeks women that are easy going, down to earth, and funny, regardless of race. He loves women that are thoughtful and caring. He said one of the most important things for any woman to know and practice is, starting the relationship the way she wants to continue it.

No Separation

Chris Denton is a 36 year-old African American man. He is single and has never been married. Chris is currently dating a 37 year-old White woman, Charley Camino. Chris was raised in a Southern Baptist Church and is also a Methodist. He was reared in a small town in Texas. Chris has two children. His girlfriend Charley has three children, and the two of them have none together. Chris's parents are both African American. They've been married for 42 years.

Chris works as a legal liaison, and Charley is a financial advisor for a large automobile company. Chris completed three years of college; Charley also completed some college. Chris and Charley met on Facebook. They began conversing and getting to know each other primarily through this social media outlet. Chris talked matter of factly about what led him away from dating Black women. He said, this includes their attitude and his having to purchase hair weaves for them which cost too much. He further explained that he's experienced more aggression from Black women, and that was just a characteristic that he was tired of dealing with. He, however, made it clear that African American women are still of interest to him, but he was interested in venturing out to different cultures.

Chris made it adamantly clear that he didn't want to be boxed in with his responses regarding the differences between Black and White women. He believes that his reason for dating outside of his race has nothing to do with race, but his simply wanting to experience something different, or perhaps create a healthy relationship with an opposite race. He explains that he's had a bad run with Black women, and it's what contributed to his wanting to try an interracial relationship.

Chris said, it's like going to the casino and consistently losing on the blue machines, eventually you have to try something different. Additionally, Chris talked openly about his need to look introspectively and gain deeper insight into himself to find clarity about his contribution to his failed relationships with African American women. Ultimately, he wants to be clear about what he brings to the table in his relationships.

Chris said in relationships and pursuits, he's not afraid of an aggressive woman, one that's willing to approach a man she's interested in. He said what he's more concerned about is how she approaches him. He'd prefer for her not to come across too strong, too open, too fast, or forward. He also believes that there are not significant differences between White and Black women. He doesn't like to categorize women based on their race differences because he feels that it perpetuates the separation of the races. He elaborated on the obvious differences, which he believes are cultural related, but not specific to race. I don't feel like there are any differences in the races other than texture, skin, or style of hair, but other than that each woman is the same, says Chris.

Chris continues to explain that the typical stereotypes that label, or are connected to Black and White women aren't always true. He said, I know some White women that are "ghetto and uneducated, just as I know some Black women, that aren't well-versed in the "black way" or that "talk white," so for me to separate the races based on stigmas or stereotypical characteristics, would go against what I believe to be true. I don't want to categorize or box women in by discussing the differences of women based on their race.

Chris believes that each man is controlled 100% by his thoughts which contributes to maintaining a positive relationship. A man's thoughts have everything to do with the type of relationship he has. How he feels about and what he thinks of his woman will ultimately be a main contributor to a positive relationship or not, says Chris. Chris explains that because society doesn't drive him, he's not swayed by any societal barriers or challenges. He's learned to not allow societal pressures or stigmatism to impact his relationship or how he feels about being a Black man dating a White woman. What Chris focuses on the most is the type of woman he's with and how to create and maintain a healthy and stable relationship. He seeks women that have humility or a sense of humor and open to trying new things. He enjoys women that are a kind of a structured free spirit; maybe this is an oxymoron, he said, but it's what he desires in a woman. Spontaneity is a big thing for him. Of course, every one wants someone pretty to look at, but that's only surface deep, Chris said. I'm kind of a simple country guy. A lot of my morals fall back on the simple things. I've been through the superficial stage, but now I look for core values and core beliefs that align with mine.

Chris said he has zero advice to give any woman about maintaining a positive relationship. He believes his opinions of that nature will only fall on deaf ears. People have to make their own way, and do what works best for them. I can only share my story, and allow people to take from it what they can, explains Chris.

Patient Love

David Tyson is a 34 year-old single male. He was born and raised in a city in Texas. Both of his parents are African American. They were never married. His biological father is deceased, and his mother is currently married to another man. David is a Christian, but is not affiliated or an active member of a church. David is dating Leslie, a 34 year-old White woman. She is also from Texas. David and Leslie have one son together and no other children. They both attended college but David didn't graduate. Leslie earned a college degree and is currently working as a real estate agent. David is temporarily not working.

David and Leslie met in college in Texas. David explained that he's dated Black women, and he was not led away from dating Black women at all. During college, Leslie was a cheerleader while he played football, and they became friends through seeing each other regularly at games and practices. They shared classes as well, and the familiarity is what persuaded him to date her. She helped him through several legal and personal challenges, and, he said, she was loyal through many difficult times. This, he explained, is what keeps him around.

David explained that if he looks back at the women that he's dated, they've mostly been mixed or white; he admits that he didn't think it was intentional, but he assumes it's the type of woman he's attracted to for a relationship. He explained that he doesn't verbally say all he wants to date are mixed or white women, but again admitted that he's generally only had substantial relationships with women that fall in this category.

At first, I didn't let her fix my plate, said Terry. She would be offended because this was something she was taught she should do for her man, Terry explained. Terry talked about his discomfort with this at first, and how it took him awhile to allow her to show him this type of love. He said he had to learn that this was a cultural thing that was different for him. Terry explains that no specific factors led him away from dating African American women. I would still date African American women tomorrow, Terry said. I could never say that I wouldn't ever date African American women again, said Terry.

As for being pursued by a woman, Terry explains that he simply wants it to be straight-forward and direct. Today, women are business owners and bosses, so it shouldn't be any mind games, Terry explained. I think one reason women become single for a long time is that they are not straight-forward in a relationship; they expect the guy to come in on a shining white horse, said Terry. Women don't say what it is they want, so I just think it's important to be open, honest and clear about what you want, Terry said.

Terry said that he doesn't feel comfortable stereotyping an entire race based on his last two relationships, but explained that he would specifically reference his two experiences. He said one main difference is the level of emotions displayed in the relationship. Casey is extremely emotional, says Terry. She also isn't afraid of being vulnerable, said Terry. Terry believes this is what contributes to a successful relationship. Casey's vulnerability opens up his comfort with being vulnerable as well. Also Terry said, communication plays a major role in their ability to sustain a healthy and positive relationship. Terry explained that the societal issues presented in their relationship mainly stemmed from his insecurities; I mean I don't know if it's more of a mental things for me, said Terry. It took me months to get comfortable with her when we were out in public, and I saw an African American woman; I always thought African American women would look down on me, or have something negative to say, he explained.

Terry also mentioned that he has never interacted with Casey's mom, which he believes is because of his race. He explained that it, however, has not put any strain on their relationship. Terry said that he's most attracted to strong women; he believes that a woman can be strong, but also sweet. He looks for the heart of the person; someone that understands the importance of treating people with the same respect that she would want. One piece of advice that he offered to African American women is to allow a man to be a man. Respect your man for who he is, and understand that he's your man not your Daddy, explained Terry.

Social Connection

Finding the right person to date and marry can mean being in the right place at the right time. Clinton Hughes, an African American man and native of Texas, became a product of his environment when he met his Mexican wife, a native of Texas and of the same age (33), at a bar. Before getting married, they dated for 2.5 years and have three children together. They have been married for eight years. Hughes earned an Associate Arts degree. He works as a firefighter paramedics with the Fire Department. His wife earned a high school diploma and works as a scale operator at a Recycle Yard.

While raised in a two-parent home and father being in the military, Hughes lived in different parts of the country such as Georgia, Texas and Germany. This experience allowed him to attend elementary and middle schools with students from different races (White, Black, Asian and Mexican) and a high school that was predominantly Black and Hispanic.

While attending high school, Hughes dated an African American woman for approximately two years. Hughes said he experienced typical problems, complaints and attitudes you can expect from a woman while in a high school relationship. The relationship was pretty crazy and not serious enough for a marriage. Occasionally, the relationship was on and off enabling Hughes to date other women. The relationship was only a title symbolizing two couples were dating each other, says Hughes.

Prior to marriage, Hughes dated a Mexican woman. This relationship lasted for about two years but was also on and off at different times. While in the relationship, Hughes said that the Mexican woman argued more than the African American woman and resulted in fighting on numerous occasions. This woman was also not a good listener regarding his concerns.

Although Hughes decided to marry a Mexican woman, he feels that he could have married an African American, Asian or White woman if the circumstances were the same where he met his wife and where he worked. All of his wife's siblings were friends of his friends. They knew and associated with the same people. Also, all of his co-workers were Mexicans.

For marriage consideration, Hughes said a woman had to have the same or similar personality as his wife such as being nice, talkative, funny and open-minded. Other personality traits he appreciates is a woman who watches football games with him, refrains from getting mad with him when he "goes out" and communicates with him where both sides are heard and understood.

Dating or marrying outside of your race can be a challenge or barrier for many couples. Since Hughes' father was in the military and came in contact with people who were in interracial marriages, Hughes did not encounter any problem from his parents for dating and marrying outside of his race. He did encounter some challenges from his cousins and friends. The women wanted to know why he was with a Mexican girl. Hughes initially addressed the concerns of people and later ignored them until the matter became obsolete.

This was not the same for Hughes wife's father. He was in total disagreement with his daughter dating and marrying an African American man. His wife's father told her not to date a Black man because he would beat her and that all Black men do is sell drugs. Since Hughes wife's parents were separated and Hughes did not meet the father until a year and a half after being together with his wife, the father had little or no influence on the their relationship, says Hughes.

Additionally, Hughes indicated that his primary challenge of being married to a Mexican woman was "in his head," so to speak. When he and his wife would go to a Mexican restaurant, he said that he would worry about the possibility of the restaurant workers "messing with his food." Hughes also said that his wife would encounter challenges on her job from co-workers. These co-workers would say things such as, "It is a sin to marry a Black man. What does your dad say about this?" According to Hughes, people say a lot of things to his wife at work, but not to them when they are together as a couple.

Whether an African American, Hispanic or Mexican woman is having a difficult time of dating or marrying, Hughes advises that a "woman should at all times respect herself, be her own woman and have an open conversation with her spouse." Listening to each other instead of reacting negatively is a key factor in any relationship.

Spiritual Connection

Lawrence Burton, a 41 year-old African American man, was born in a city in Georgia, and is married. He and his wife, Sasha, have been married for seven years. Sasha is also a Georgia native, and an Arab. Lawrence's dad is Black and his Mom is Arab; they have been married for 47 years. Lawrence explains that he doesn't associate himself with a specific religion but considers himself as a spiritual being. Lawrence and Sasha have two children together. Lawrence has a bachelor's degree and graduated from a historically Black college. He currently works in education. His wife is a social media journalist, and also attended and graduated from college.

Lawrence met Sasha at a club in North Georgia. I think in my last relationship, we were just too young. We were both pursuing careers, and I think our passions just got in the way of our marriage, explains Lawrence. Lawrence was married two years to an African American woman; however, the marriage ended in divorce due to irreconcilable differences. Lawrence couldn't identify one specific reason why he chose to stop dating Black women. He explains that he had no intention to just stop dating Black women, but met his wife, and fell in love with her.

He explains that he is very attracted to African American women, and has no specific body size preference. I like all proportions, he says. You could be skinny and shapely or you could be thick and shapely. As for complexion, it doesn't matter to me. My first wife was darker complexioned, and my current wife is lighter complexioned, says Lawrence. He explains that he's more concerned with energy or vibe, and how it aligns. The goals of a woman and personality type are most important, and this is what makes a good relationship, says Lawrence.

I wouldn't say that I have any reservations about Black women, but I will say that in my experience, the history of Black women in general tends to mold certain reactions to things that happen, which is not to handle situations in a mild mannered way, says Lawrence. He explains that it is understood why sisters act this way. They have been through a lot throughout history, which has taught them to stand up and be strong. This can become a knee jerk reaction instead of a tool, says Lawrence.

Some factors that led me to marry outside of my race were the different concepts about money and gender roles. Lawrence makes certain to mention that he treads lightly on this subject, and explains that his wife, for example, has been trained to be more docile. Lawrence explains that he doesn't take advantage of this, but he does enjoy it, says Lawrence. There are some Black women like this, but it's not a cultural thing. Black women are brought up to be strong and independent. I'm saying this isn't a bad thing, but it doesn't foster the attitude for women to recognize a good man.

Lawrence jokes about wanting expensive gifts and jewelry when being pursued by a woman, but then explains that really just being a considerate person is important to him. Lawrence says he also wants someone who can recognize his needs and know what he likes or what turns him on. Being married to a Black woman was different because she would do all the duties of a wife, until she was mad at me. Then it all stopped. But, with my current wife, there's no stipulation on what she generally does as a wife, just because she's mad or we're having some type of disagreement.

Being able to let go, knowing that you can't change a person is paramount in successful relationships. In my marriage with an Arab, I have to be open culturally and sensitive to her cultural rituals and routines in order to maintain a positive relationship. Because Sasha is Muslim, and I'm not, this poses major spiritual and family barriers. But, when we met, there was such great chemistry, and we got along so well. I couldn't be without her, Lawrence explains. We had easy communication. This is what I always look for in a woman, and that is what I found in my wife.

Lawrence recommends women to find some way to be friends with the man before dating, or thoroughly vet the guy. Be friends first though; most people tell who they are through friendship. You get a true sense of the person's character by being friends first.

Superficial Mentalities

Joey Douglas is a 37 year-old single African American man from a city in Michigan. He currently lives in a city in California. He was raised by his mother and had no relationship with his biological father. He is not religious, but does consider himself a spiritual being. Joey has no children. He's dating Claire a 30 year-old White woman from a city in California. Joey attended a historically Black college in Florida where he studied Business Administration. He currently works in sales at a car dealership in California. Claire also works in sales at the same dealership. They both also aspire to act, and often create funny skits that they post on social media about typical relationship issues.

Joey and Claire met at work. Their relationship is more of a strong friendship, he said. What connects the two of them is their interest in acting and making people laugh. Joey explained that he has dated outside of his race, but doesn't have a preference of race when he pursues a woman. He said, he dates whomever he is interested in at the time. He talked about the struggles of dating and maintaining longevity in a relationship in California. So many of the women out here have superficial mentalities about relationships. It's like a movie, or everybody wants a movie lifestyle, he said.

A few of the skits he and Claire have filmed poke fun at these types of women and relationships. It's an epidemic, he said. Women out here are looking to be "kept," (taken care of) and the majority of men are average, they don't make enough to take care of a woman like that, said Joey.

Joey didn't have any factors that led him away from dating Black women. He explained that he dates everybody; or anybody that he sees fit or is his type of woman. Joey said he doesn't have a certain type, but he does like women who have a sense of humor. Because he works fulltime and is pursuing his acting career, he looks for women who understand that his time is limited.

Claire gets my "hustle," said Joey. We click because she's in my same "lane," he said. Joey noticed that the friendship that he and Claire has makes the relationship better. I don't put stipulations on the relationship, and neither does she, he said. We just go with the flow, said Joey. This works for us. I'm not sure how many sisters would honestly be able to handle this scenario, Joey explained. We are friends first, so we can disagree about things, and still make the relationship work.

He also talked about the relationship being a friendship that can withstand a breakup. Even if we don't make it as a couple per se, I think we'll always be friends, said Joey. That's rare, he said. Joey also said that he likes bold women. So, if he's ever to be approached, he wants it to always be memorable. I'm a comedian and actor, so I like a scene, he said. Women don't typically approach me, so if they do, I want her to go all out with an introduction. I want it to be no confusion or question about her wanting me, he said.

To be honest, regardless of race, with everybody that I'm with, I like to be friends first. That's really important to me, especially now that I've experienced it with Claire, Joey said. People are afraid to cross the boundaries as friends, but it can work if both people are open to it, he said.

Joey said the biggest challenge in the friendship with Claire is the amount of time they spend together, both working together and working on their film projects. We are around each other a lot, he said. So, we have to give each other a break from each other so we don't get tired of each other. Joey said he seeks women who are cool, laid back and down to earth. He likes women who have a good sense of humor and can take a joke. As long as she has a sense of humor and attractive, I am satisfied, said Joey. Oh, and she can't be crazy, he said. I need a mentally stable woman in my life, Joey joked.

Joey's advice to Black women is not be so serious all the time. Take a joke! Laugh a little, he said.

Tickled Fancy

Tommy Owen is a 36 year-old married African American man. He's from New Jersey and has been married for two years. Both of his parents are Black and have been married for 32 years. Tommy is a Baptist Christian. His wife Cherry is a 27 year-old White woman. She's from Massachusetts. The two of them have two children together. Tommy works as an Education Investigator for a public school district in New York, and Cherry is a Special Education teacher in the same school district. They both have college degrees.

Tommy and Cherry met at work. He has also dated African American women in the past; however, his last marriage was to a woman that's not black. There weren't really any factors that led Tommy away from Black women, Tommy explains. But it was just at the time that Cherry just "tickled my fancy." I didn't set out looking for a White woman, it just happened, Tommy says.

Tommy explains that he doesn't have a preference for any particular type of woman. There are no specific laws of attraction for him. I like Black women period, he says. Hair is hair to Tommy. I've had girls with a whole bunch of hair and some with none. He explains that what's most important is how they treat him. Whoever is nicest to me, I roll with, Tommy says. Now, when I was about 14, I went through a light skinned phase. But I think girls also had affection toward light-skinned boys during the 1990s. Artists like Genuwine made it hard for dark skinned brothers, said Tommy.

Tommy explains that he really never had any complexes. I always thought I'd be with an African American woman, he says. I really never thought I'd be in the situation I'm in now, Tommy explains. Tommy had no reservations about Black women; he said that he has no qualms with Black women at all.

Tommy couldn't pinpoint a specific reason that led him to marry a White woman. I don't really know. I just did it. One day I was like she's nice, she helped me out, and bent over backwards helping me to succeed. Nobody really did anything like that for me before, so I rolled with it. My mom always told me she never had a problem with me dating outside my race, as long as they treat me well, so I always rolled with that, says Tommy.

Tommy talked about his ideal pursuit from a woman. I like women that make the first move, but in no particular way. I come with no expectations, says Tommy. Tommy has noticed a few cultural differences in his relationship. If I'm watching the television show Martin, she may not get it, or also like different foods, she's never experienced, he says. It's not too much more, but a few cultural differences, Tommy explains. He said she pretty much asks me, if it's something she's uncomfortable with, or doesn't understand. So, not too many cultural differences that come to play in their relationship, said Tommy.

We don't have any challenges, but we see the stigma sometimes, says Tommy. We'll walk sometimes and Black women will glare at me or at her. But we understand that it comes with the territory; it's an occupational hazard. But, she gets the same types of reactions from White people when she's by herself, says Tommy. She told me the other day, she was in the mall, a White woman approached her, and asked if our daughter was hers. She gets that a lot, says Tommy.

Tommy explains that he's generally a laid back person. He's learned not to let a lot bother him, which helps to contribute to maintaining a positive relationship. The world has changed a lot, Tommy said, and I'm starting to see more and more interracial children and people, Tommy says.

Tommy explained that he's attracted to educated women. He said, I'm not saying she has to be a college graduate, but she has to have a level of intelligence to hold a conversation. I like to talk politics.

He also wants his woman to be attractive, nice, and fun. I don't ask for much, he says. Tommy didn't have many words of advice to African American women seeking to date or marry an African American man, but said it's important to just be you.

Troubled Paradise

Bentley Jackson is a 36 year-old African American man. He's currently married, but separated from his wife. Both of his parents are African Americans. They are divorced from each other, but both have remarried. Bentley's wife is an African American woman; however, he is currently dating Suzette, a White woman. Suzette is 27 years old and has one child. Bentley has two children with his estranged wife.

Suzette and Bentley don't have any children together. Bentley and Suzette are from a city in Texas. They both have high school diplomas, and did not attend college. Bentley works a night shift for a manufacturing company and met Suzette at work.

Bentley explained that nothing specifically stopped him from dating Black women. I don't discriminate, says Bentley. I've always loved them all. It doesn't really matter. I ended up marrying a Black chick, and now I'm dating a White one, says Bentley. I really like dark skinned women. I like long hair and shapely Black women, Bentley explains.

Bentley further explained that his marriage to a Black woman was a struggle based on personality differences. Bentley also admitted to acts of infidelity that also put a serious strain on trust and communication in his relationship.

I'm not really sure how I'd want to be pursued; I guess just with a person that's real and honest about how she feels, said Bentley. I honestly haven't noticed too many differences in my two relationships, other than maybe physical characteristics, like skin textures. White women have a different skin elasticity than Black women, said Bentley. Often times, when we're out, I've experienced harsh looks from both Black and White people. No one has ever been bold enough to approach us, but I've been in a few uncomfortable situations, based on our race differences, Bentley said.

Women are women. I honestly don't think there were many differences that involve race. Our challenges mostly involved trust, Bentley admits. My perspective of relationships has changed; I'm older and look for different qualities than I did in the past, said Bentley. Bentley describes the qualities of a woman that are most important to him such as honesty, compassion, inside and outer beauty, and patience.

Bentley said that the best advice that he could give is simply for women to know what they want, and to not settle for less.

Turned Off

Barry Carlos is a single 36 year-old African American man. He is dating Susan, a 36 year-old White woman. Barry has never been married. His parents are both African Americans and are divorced; however, his father is now deceased, and his Mother never remarried.

Barry was raised as a Baptist Christian; he has one son, who is mulatto. Barry is no longer dating his son's mother, who is also a

White woman. Barry and Susan were both born in a city in Texas. He and Susan are high school graduates and completed some college. Neither of the two graduated. Susan also has one child.

Barry met Susan in high school, which is where they initially started dating. Barry said that he has dated African American women in the past, but says that he chooses to date who he's most attracted to, which are White women. Barry attributes the reason for not being attracted to or interested in Black women due to their not being attracted to him in his teens. They didn't like my dark skin, he said. I have never really hit it off with Black women. It is always been a friend thing, never anything romantic, says Barry.

Barry talked candidly about his need for attention in the relationship. He believes that communication is key to maintaining a healthy relationship. I must know that the woman is interested in me. But, my number one law of attraction is attraction, says Barry. Call me shallow or whatever, but I have to be attracted to her. He continued by adding that his number two priority is attention or high levels of interest. Talking, calling, and consistent texting during the dating phase is a necessity for me, says Barry.

Barry expressed that body size isn't a deal breaker for him, but he's expecting whomever the woman is, regardless of size, to be attractive. As for body size, her body must be fine, he says. Fine can be different sizes, she just needs to be fine, Barry exclaims. Honestly, I think Black women are more comfortable or okay with being a little bigger, explains Barry. Other women get to a certain size, and they do something about it, but Black women don't really do the same. As for hair, says Barry, I'm a natural guy. Barry says he's not into the fake hair at all. It's not really a deal breaker, he says, but I don't like it. Barry also explains that although he is mainly attracted to White women, he is also attracted to brown-skinned Black women. I know this may seem weird, he says. Maybe you thought since I'm mainly attracted to White women, I might like light skinned Black girls, but nah I'm attracted to brown skinned women too, says Barry.

Barry passionately expressed his concern or reservation with Black women. My main reservation is on a grander scale regarding Black women; it's just I don't think they are nice people. Maybe I'm wrong, but I just don't think they are nice people. And, I really don't have to date them to know this, says Barry. I see it at work, and I am around them all the time. They aren't pleasant. They don't speak, if you don't know them, explains Barry. Having a pleasant personality is a critical characteristic Barry seeks in his women, as he explains this is not a quality he has noticed in most Black women.

I date outside my race because I like pleasant, nice, and happy go lucky type of women. That's why I don't generally date Black women, says Barry. Barry talked briefly about societal pressures and disapproval. He said, I find that people often get uncomfortable when we are in certain places. I am use to the uncomfortable looks, but it doesn't bother me anymore, he explains.

Barry had trouble with explaining how he would like for a woman to pursue him. He adamantly believes that only rich men are approached or pursued by women. I couldn't even answer that question, I have no idea, says Barry. I don't know what guys that's happening to, maybe guys with money. I couldn't even answer that question, I have no idea, says Barry.

Barry explains that it's hard to differentiate between African American and White women because he's never dated a Black woman. I've "kicked it" with them, but not really seriously dated them. I think I'd probably be nervous about what I'm supposed to do, if I dated a Black woman. I mean, I know what White girls like, but not really sure about Black women, Barry explains.

Barry says that being positive and attentive is what makes any relationship work. I look for a calm and nice type of woman. The advice he offers to Black women is to simply, be nicer.

Young Love

Raymond Miller is a 19 year-old African American man; he's never been married and has no children. Both of Raymond's parents are African American, and they've been married for 20 plus years. Raymond is a Baptist Christian. He was born in a city in Illinois. He's currently serving in the Air Force and is based in Illinois. His White girlfriend Alana is also 19; she is studying to be a nurse and currently working in cosmetology. She has no children. Raymond met Alana in a Spanish class during their 9th grade year of high school. He explained that they immediately hit it off. She had a great personality, said Raymond.

Raymond said that there weren't any specific factors that led him away from African American women. He explained that the neighborhood he grew up in and the schools he attended simply didn't have many African American girls. So, he was attracted to the girls that he was around the most. Raymond mentioned dating an African American girl during his middle school years, but couldn't recall any specific factors or personality traits that made the relationship any different. I've always been around more White than Black people, said Raymond. I don't think it had anything to do with not wanting to date an African American person; there just aren't many in my town, he explained.

Raymond said he's attracted to women with long hair, but that doesn't mean he's opposed to short hair. He also said he prefers fit women, who enjoy working out. Raymond explained that staying in shape and going to the gym regularly is something he and Alana have in common. If ever he were to date anyone else, that's a quality he prefers. He's also attracted to women with beautiful skin, women that are smart and can hold a conversation, he said. Raymond said one reservation he has with women, not particularly African American women, but women in general is becoming comfortable too fast. He said he likes them to move at a natural pace, but sometimes women push things along faster than he would like. My relationship has been positive so far, said Raymond. Alana and my parents are really close. They often have family nights together, Raymond explained.

Furthermore, Raymond said, there's no tension between the races. And, in his neighborhood, its common to see interracial relationships, so he's never felt discriminated against, nor has he been in an uncomfortable situation.

Real Stories of Why African American Women Jump to Date or Marry White Men

African American women are dating or marrying outside of their race at a rate significantly lower than African American men who are dating or marrying outside of their race. In 2010, for example, 168,000 Black women were married to White men compared to 390,000 Black men married to White women in the same year. The following provides an except of interviews from several African American women to explore why African American women jump to date or marry White men. For confidentiality, the names have been changed.

Broader Perspective

Laura Hoskins is a single 36 year-old African American woman; she was born in a city in Illinois. Both of Laura's parents are African American. Laura explained that her parents have been legally married for over 30 years, but have been separated for at least half of those years. Laura considers herself a Christian, and was raised primarily within the same religious denomination. Her Mom has not initiated a divorce, and has never remarried. Neither has her Dad. Laura has never been married.

Although Laura is originally from Illinois, she's lived in Texas for the majority of her child and adult life. Laura's currently dating Tim, a

White 62 year-old man. Tim was born and raised in a city in Texas. They both currently reside in a city in Texas. Both Laura and Tim attended and graduated from college. From a previous marriage, Tim has three adult children; however, Laura has no children. Laura worked primarily in retail banking, but recently switched to underwriting of loans. Tim owns and operates a successful commercial refrigeration business.

Tim and Laura met at a retail bank she managed. Tim was a client of Laura's, and the two of them developed a friendly yet business rapport in the beginning stages of their relationship. The relationship began to change much later, explains Laura. Laura stated that she's primarily dated African American men throughout her life. She said that Tim was the total opposite of what she anticipated her man to look like. He came in a totally different package, said Laura. Laura couldn't identify any particular factors that led her away from dating Black men. In fact, she always assumed she would be with a Black man. She dated one Black man for several years, and just could never get him to fully commit. However, she never anticipated or sought to date outside of her race.

I thought I had a particular type of man that I was not interested or attracted to, but now I've realized that none of those stereotypes or particulars matters, said Laura. What matters is how one treats, respects and values you. That's what's attractive to me now, Laura explained. She also felt like there weren't any particular personality traits or personality characteristics that she could identify about the African American man, because she explained that each African American man she dated was different. She didn't want to label or stereotype Black men based solely on her experiences. She did, however, mention that the difference in her current relationship is age. Tim is mature, and has "been there, done that," so to speak. He knows exactly what he wants, and values every moment we're together, said Laura. I have no reservations about African American men; I'm happy in my relationship, but only because of the person

Tim is, said Laura. I wanted Black love, but my man (Tim) came in a totally different package, Laura stated.

Laura talked briefly about her perspective of the laws of attraction; I like an approach that is matter-of-fact, straight-forward, honest and without game. I want a man that knows what he wants, period, said Laura. When approaching me, I want an assured man, Laura explained. She also explained that this matter-of-fact approach was what attracted her to Tim. She explained that she had no intention to date an older White man, but he was such a gentleman. He treated me so well, and I felt like I could always be my true self around him, Laura stated. In comparison to other relationships, the only difference Laura discussed was the genuine interest that Tim exhibited, and that Tim was very clear about his intentions with her. I never have to guess if he wants me or is in my corner. He always shows me how much he cares and wants to be with me, Laura stated. She also contributed this quality to him being an older man, and having had many experiences in life.

Laura further explained that one main factor that contributes to a positive relationship is being open-minded. Tim's friends and inner-circle aren't always accepting of me. People assume that I'm with him for his money, and this is sometimes difficult, Laura explained. So, I often have to maintain an open-mind when I'm around them, said Laura.

Dating outside your race is equally as challenging as dating within your race. People have to be willing to bend, and not be so set on a specific type of man, said Laura. My suggestion for women is to keep an open-mind because you never know what size, color or body type your soul mate might come in, Laura stated. I've learned to honestly not even see color, through this relationship; I totally just see the person. I know this sounds cliche, but it is the truth, stated Laura.

Christian Faith

Just like a needle lost in a haystack, many people are lost about the real reason for Colin Kaepernick and other National Football League's (NFL) players kneeling during the National Anthem. Erica Simpson, a 49 year-old African American woman who is married to a 55 year-old White man, experienced first hand how her husband (Clark Letterman) did not understand the reason for the inequalities experienced by African Americans. In sharing with her husband an incident of a police officer sitting on an African American man's back and still shooting him point blank, the first question her husband raised was, isn't it illegal to sell CD's outside a store? Erica angrily responded to her husband, this is what's wrong with White America. Rather than being outraged and ask me is the man dead or alive, you want to find a reason the police shot the man in the back, says Erica.

Because of Erica's life experience and maturity, she was able to help Clark become aware of racial inequalities and particularly see the injustices in America from an African American perspective. Before Clark met Erica, he would ignore acts of racism. Now, he takes a stand in his own way as result of her influence. According to Erica, her husband says he is seeing things on race relations better through her eyes.

In 2011, Erica and Clark met through an online dating website called eHarmony. eHarmony matches single women and men with each other for long-term relationships. In completing the profile information with eHarmony, Erica's focus was to find a man, regardless of race, who was geared towards her Christian faith and had integrity. Ironically, Clark, residing in his native state (Ohio) was looking for the same qualities in a woman. He had been in a 19 year marriage that ended in a bitter divorce due to his wife's infidelity. He waited five years after the divorce before contacting eHarmony to find his perfect match.

Erica, a native of Mississippi who was residing in Illinois, had dated White men who praised her complexion, beauty, speech and intelligence. These men were secure with themselves and had no issue with her hair, says Erica. However, family members of these men opposed interracial dating which subsequently kept their relationships from growing.

Erica had also dated African American men before her online dating experience. These men were insecure and uncommitted to a serious long-term relationship. Their interest was more about using her for a "booty call" and moving on to the next woman. Collectively, these men denigrated her for not having a "butt or curves," cutting her hair from long to short and refusing to have sex with them when they wanted it, says Erica. So she sought eHarmony to have access to a larger selection of men and "weed out" the perpetrators, says Erica.

With Erica and Clark residing in different cities and having a similar focus for dating as presented on their eharmony profile, they started talking by telephone, which enabled them to talk and listen to each other and subsequently confirm their mutual interest, says Erica. In 2013, they met in person. Clark, a college graduate and manager for a non-profit company, proposed to Erica one month after their first date. While squandering no time, they married eight months later and currently have been married for four years.

As part of the marriage, Erica a college graduate and auditor for a nonprofit organization, eagerly accepted the commitment of helping Clark raise his four children from his former marriage. With Clark feeling bad about his divorce and children coming out of a broken home, he neglected parenting skills and gave the children everything they asked for without their having to do anything. This became a challenge for the marriage, says Erica. However, through Clark's cooperation, Erica was able to instill in the children that you have to do some chores such as cleaning the house and taking out the trash to earn things you want in life.

Having someone who truly loves you and tells you that on a daily basis is awesome, says Erica. I am fortunate to be in a marriage where people respect me at church although I am the only African American person. Also, people in Clark's family respect me as well. I have not faced any opposition from people in the community where we reside in Ohio as a married couple. Our Christian faith has consistently and positively kept our relationship together, says Erica.

For a woman who is seeking to date a man and maintain a positive relationship with him, Erica suggests that she: (1) be secure in who you are; (2) have your own goals established and (3) find someone who matches with your focus or goals in life. Erica says, if a woman has to change her goals to be with the man, this probably is not going to work. In fact, I did not go on eharmony looking for a White man, but a man who would match my goals and find me to be his wife, says Erica.

In the past, I was limited to meeting men in my circle such as the grocery store, work, church and through my girl friends. At the same time, I was looking for a certain type of man. I dated African American men, for instance, who were very handsome, tall and fine. My husband does not possess the physique that I would have normally looked for in a man, but the way he loves me is what got me. He tells me on a daily basis that he loves me; and he allows me to be an equal partner with him, says Erica.

From Then to Now

Tiffany Buttons is a 36 year-old married African American woman. Tiffany was born in a city in Missouri, but was raised in a city in Texas. She's been married for two years to Ian Buttons. Both of Tiffany's parents are African Americans; neither of them is currently married. Tiffany is a Baptist Christian; both she and her husband are members and actively involved in a Mega Church in Texas. Ian, a White man, is also 36 year-old; he was born and raised in a city in Texas. The two of them have one child together, and Tiffany has one child from a previous relationship. Tiffany and Ian are both college educated. She works in banking as a branch manager, and Ian is a personal body guard to a celebrity public figure.

Tiffany and Ian met when they were teenagers at church. They dated for awhile, but as they grew older, drifted apart. They found their way back to each other through social media. Tiffany said that she has dated Black men most of her dating life, outside of the time she dated Ian during high school. I think trust was a major factor for me; I'm not sure if that has anything to do with race, but it played a major part in my past relationship, said Tiffany.

Tiffany explained that although she had struggles with Black men and trust issues, if she weren't married, she more than likely would date other Black men. Ian just came at the right time, and filled in the missing pieces for me, said Tiffany. It wasn't about race, but who he is as a man, said Tiffany. He was just the fresh breath of air I needed, she said. Black men are beautiful; they're broken, many of them anyway, but beautiful creations; so I can't really think of any particular reservations about the race as a whole.

However, there are many similar issues concerning the lack of trust that I don't appreciate, said Tiffany. Loyalty and trust go hand-in-hand, and in my last relationship, I faced several infidelity issues that made it hard for me to trust. However, again, I'm not really sure this has all to do with race, or if it's a personality trait, Tiffany said.

Tiffany talked candidly about her relationship, the joys, highs and lows that accompanied it. She explained that this relationship, although with a White man, was not particularly different than with a Black man, outside of skin tone. She talked about having to adjust, and work through differences, just as she had in her previous relationships with

Black men. She explained that she married outside of her race simply because Ian was the right man for her. He supports me, said Tiffany.

Tiffany couldn't identify any particular way that she'd like a man to pursue her, but if any way, she wants it to be straight forward and without game, so to speak. The differences in her marriage with a White man, had more to do with cultural differences, and some pertained to personality differences. Culturally, Ian and I had different upbringings, but we liked the same music, food, and just have a lot of similarities, so it didn't take too much adjusting, said Tiffany. She explained that the differences weren't as prevalent between them because they also knew each other when they were young. So, they were familiar with each other, which made their dating as adults more comfortable.

I think with any relationship, there's a getting to know phase, where you just have to get to know each other, said Tiffany. This isn't related to race at all, she said. I think the most challenging part about introducing your man, that isn't Black, to friends and family is their initial reaction, said Tiffany. I honestly think once I accepted that race wasn't an issue, everyone else around me did too, she said. I've never experienced any blatant racism from strangers; I don't think I was ever willing to see it either, said Tiffany. Other people's opinions don't impact me at all, she said. And, my husband does an amazing job protecting us, Tiffany said.

I love strong-willed and determined men; men that have a plan, and steps to accomplish them, said Tiffany. I, of course, also want an honest man, a God-fearing man, and one who has the capacity to love selflessly, said Tiffany. I think women should first be clear about what they want before seeking to date. Be prepared to communicate and be open and truthful with their significant other. Don't carry baggage into new relationships. This applies to dating any man whether they are White, Black, purple or blue, said Tiffany.

Key Advice from African American Men

Many African American women are seeking to date or marry an African American man and maintain a positive relationship with him. The following provides a summary of the advice from African American men to African American women grouped by category.

Attitude

- Take a good look at your behavior; relinquish the 'me, me attitude' or syndrome. If you are in a marriage, allow it to be mutual: don't let your demands be all about materialistic things. (Best Friends)
- Don't be loud and vociferous; don't go in the public trying to be seen by everybody; focus on your man. Be gentle and kind and don't be confrontational. Act or play your part in the relationship. Be peaceful in your behavior; don't show it negatively in the public. (Best Friends)
- Get rid of the anger and maintain a positive mental attitude in pursuit of your interests. When you have so much anger ingrained inside of you, it stops your growth emotionally, socially and spiritually. (Comfort Level)
- Have and maintain a positive attitude in a relationship. Believe in your man; don't jump to conclusions about things, put your man down or give up on him and be willing to listen to the man before you react on something. (Military Love)

- Stand by your man, be supportive, trusting, trustworthy, and open to try new things and learn to agree to disagree. (Awkward Mix)
- Black women have taken this independent thing and turned it into a cop-out to not fulfill their matrimonial and parenting duties. Everybody has rules in life and I don't mean that you're to be somebody's door mat but there's a certain level of submissiveness that's allowed and necessary. Be submissive. (Foreign Interest)
- Be nicer. (Turned Off)

Appearance

- Whatever attracted you or your mate to the relationship such as physical appearance, maintain that appearance. Find an exercise program that works for you and helps to maintain your health. This helps to stimulate interest and intimacy in the relationship. (Body Type)
- Be who you are in the relationship. Don't start adding wigs or artificial hair to look like someone else (Body Type)

Expectations

- Be how you are and allow the man to be who he is. In doing so, you can see who the person is and decide if you want to be with him (Country Boy)
- Be patient with your man and learn to listen (Curiosity)
- Stop thinking that every African American man must fit a certain profile in order to be in a relationship with him. Be open to the African American man's background, history and lifestyle and allow him to be who he is and not someone else. (Body Type)
- Stop being selective or particular in choosing an African American man; stop setting your standards too high and

undermining the value of a blue-collar worker. (Limited Supply)

- Allow a man to be a man; respect your man for who he is and understand he is your man and not your daddy. (Pleasantly Surprised)
- Be independent but let the man be the man. That doesn't mean women need to be barefoot and pregnant in a kitchen but simply should step back and allow a man to take care of the household. (Attitude Matters)
- Let go some of the control and learn to relax. Enjoy the time. Sometimes Black women look for unrealistic qualities in men and should reevaluate the qualities that are important to them. (Patient Love)

Friends

- Stop looking for a man and find a friend; get to know him as a person and be patient in the process (Man Attraction)
- Find some way to be friends with the man before dating or thoroughly vet the guy. Most people tell who they are through friendship. You get a true sense of the person's character by being friends first. (Spiritual Connection)
- Make it about your values rather than race. Understand your values and make sure your values align with the person you are in a relationship with. (Mother's Influence)
- Get to know the man and determine if he is the right person for you. Don't immediately jump in bed with him. Try to enjoy each other first. Take it slow. (My Angel)
- Be a shoulder for your man and create a space at home that is of peace and not stress. (No Animosity)

Secrets

- Don't share your man's personal business with your girlfriends. No man wants to feel like he is dating you and all of your girlfriends at the same time. (Body Type)
- Think before you put certain "words out there in the streets" about your man. (Life's Perspective)

Confidence

- Remain confident in yourself and avoid becoming angry about interracial couples. (Jonathan Dickerson)
- Women who love themselves and are more confident in themselves make great partners. (Love Oneself)
- Be more patient and confident in yourself (Color Complex)
- Be open-minded. Don't be afraid to try other things. Enjoy life. (Not Black Enough)
- Don't be so serious all the time. Take a joke! Laugh a little. (Superficial Mentalities)
- Black women are too uptight sometimes. Chill out, just chill out. Everything isn't the end of the world. (A Break)
- Be encouraged and set goals with your man. Know where you want to be in ten years and try to reach milestones with the man you are with. Instead of just being focused on having a good time, get to know what he wants out of life and compare his wants and goals to yours. (Always Positive)
- Remain sexually active in the relationship. Don't forget this is important in a relationship. Be proactive rather than reactive in having sex with your mate. (Body Type)

Key Advice from African American Women

The following is advice from the African American women interviewed who are dating or married to White men.

- Keep an open mind because you never know that size, color or body type your soul mate might come in. (Broader Perspective)
- Be secure in who you are. Have your own goals established and find someone who matches with your focus or goals in life. If you have to change your goals to be with a man, this is probably not going to work. (Christian Faith)
- Be clear about what you want before seeking to date. Be prepared to communicate and be open and truthful with your significant other. Don't carry baggage into new relationships. (From Then to Now)

Advice from a Matchmaker

While on a cruise, Speaker Julie Wadley, a personal match-maker and coach for Black women, provided tips for understanding the stages in which "men think" with regard to choosing a date and marrying a woman. The following provides an excerpt of Wadley's four key points.

Stage I

When a man is choosing a mate, the woman must be attractive to him. The man likes certain attributes of a woman whether physical or non-physical; so you must stay healthy and conscious of your body because he is always looking. You also have to be interesting or stimulating to him. You must keep a little mystery, keep confidence in who you are, show respect for yourself and be conscious of what you want, says Wadley.

Stage 2

Once the man is attracted to you, he must know you are his friend especially when he is faced with challenges in life. Some critical concerns the man has about a possible mate are, "Can you share an interest with him?" Can you keep a secret? Can you blend in well in his life? Are you independent? Can he trust you? Can he take you places and not encounter any problems? A man wants to be proud to introduce you to people in his circle if you are the chosen one.

You have to understand what motivates him and makes him feel safe and secure, says Wadley.

Stage 3

At this stage, you have been chosen and become a friend with a man. In order to become family, you must gain his trust. You are in the inner circle if you can predict what he wants before he asks you. At this point, he is ready to make decisions with you in mind. The man may become inquisitive in asking a question such as "Does she want children?" If yes, that's a good thing for him, says Wadley.

Stage 4

Being faithful (fidelity) is the pinnacle to the man being in a relationship with a woman. The man tries to protect his heart and be very careful with whom he lets inside of him. He will commit when he is ready to commit with you. Actually, he has to image his life with you; so you must be able to add to his life rather than take from his life. You must bring value to the relationship in order for him to totally commit to you, says Wadley.

Similarly, the following provides an excerpt of six elements on "how to make anyone fall in love with you" according to Lowndes (1996).

Element 1 First Impressions

When you first meet a person, there are numerous reactions that might take place. This might include your mind functioning like a computer and thinking about how you are going to act or communicate on your first date.

Element 2 Similar Character

There should be some similarities or commonalities if a person is to be together with another person for a lifespan. Your heart seeks for a person who has similar characters, beliefs, values, etc. as yours. Your heart seeks to find a person who enjoys going to activities of your interest so you can have fun together. Also, your heart seeks to find a person who can do things you are unfamiliar with or have not experienced.

Elements 3 Equity

In a long-term relationship, each person is looking for value. Each person wants to know "What IS In It For Me (WIIFM)?" So, it is critical for each person to convince the other person that you are getting value or a good deal in the relationship. At the same time, each person is assessing or asking the critical question, "Is this the best offer I can get from such relationship?"

Element 4 Ego

The core of romance is ego. A person falls in love with another person if that person has the ideal reflections of himself or herself.

Element 5 Early-Date, Gender-Menders

Since a man and woman communicate and think in different ways, it is essential for a potential couple to understand this and use the knowledge about each other's styles and personalities to his or her advantage.

Element 6 Rx for Sex—How to Turn on the Sexual Electricity

While a man might engage in sex with his mate in different ways and extended periods of time and a woman might possess a huge breast and curvy shape to entice her mate, it is essential for the man and woman to understand that the "brain is the most exotic organ in the body. The mind power is what drives the mighty machine and keeps it generating heat for many years" in a relationship. For the man, the focus should be on the passion and sexuality he creates in the relationship and the sensation he exuberates to his mate each time he sees her. For the woman, the focus should be on her sexual attitude and how she deals with her mate's individual sexuality in the relationship rather than size of her body parts.

Excerpt of Spiritual Advice from a Minister

While attending a worship service at Bethel Baptist Institutional Church in Jacksonville, Florida, Bishop Rudolph McKissick Jr. spoke on the subject, "I found my happy place." As a reference for the subject, McKissick cited Matthew Chapter 5 verse 1: And seeing the multitudes, he went up into a mountain: and when he was set, his disciples came unto him: And he opened his mouth, and taught them saying, Blessed are the poor in spirit: for theirs is the kingdom of heaven (King James Version, Holy Bible).

According to McKissick, people can find their "happy place" when they repent and give their life to Jesus Christ. You don't look for material things or people to make you happy. The only thing that can give you constant happiness is a mind change through Jesus Christ. When you are happy through Jesus Christ, you can go to sleep happy and awake in the morning happy despite your trials and tribulations. You may be broke, unemployed, single or divorced but through Jesus Christ you can be happy. Through Him, your mind will be shifted to disallow anything to steal your joy. You must remember that "this joy I have, the world did not give it to me; and the world can not take it from me," says McKissick.

People, however, look for happiness in the wrong places, says McKissick. They look for happiness in houses, money, power, positions, degrees and prestige. They look for happiness in the skin complexion and body size of individuals. In fact, they spend an insurmountable amount of time looking for mates that are of perfect dimensions, and they discover that the mates have too much baggage to make them happy.

Thus, people can never be happy if they don't have a connection with Jesus Christ. Having a relationship with Christ allows you to view, analyze and understand life from a different perspective, says McKissick.

CONCLUSION

Writing this book has been a 16 month endeavor although I avoided the topic for three years. I had reservations about how it might be perceived by African Americans and other ethnic groups. I did not want to create further tension among the races.

As a researcher, I began this topic with the idea of learning why African American men date or marry women outside of their race. This question was formulated from seeing an increasing number of Black men who seemed comfortable with this status. It was also a question that I found was on the minds of our African American women and creating a sort of anger and concern about their chances of meeting the Black man of their dreams.

While this small study did gain some answers, it also opened and presented other questions. Considering the insurgence of interracial couples in the U.S. coupled with the shortage of available African American men, what are African American women going to do?

Contrary to popular beliefs, morals and values, many African American women may have to decide if it is time for them to "jump the fence." They may find that waiting patiently for the "right man" within their race may never occur. They may find that the odds are against them due to the number of African American men who are incarcerated, uneducated or unemployed. They may also find that lowering their standards to be with a man within their race is absolutely absurd and asinine.

It is my hope that this book will inspire women of all races and nationalities to date whomever they choose without compromising their lifestyles or standards to do so. It is my hope that our African

American sisters will do as others and begin to expand their dating and marriage options by taking advantage of their rights to date and marry whomever they choose. Thus, it is my hope that people will see the value of the book and improve their relationships with their mates and find their happiness in life.

REFERENCES

Balwit, N. (2017). The urban-rural divide in interracial marriage. Retrieved September 30, 2017 from https://www.citylab.com/equity/2017/05/interracial-marriage-in-cities-pew-report/527217/

Berry, C.D. & Duke, B. (2011). Explores a deep-seated bias within Black Culture against women with darker skin. Dark Girls Film. King James Version. Holy Bible.

Brown, Stacy M. (2013). Interracial dating gains popularity online. Washington Informer, 49, 29-30.

Christopher, E. L. (2015). The love and marriage playbook: Contemporary guidelines for black women in relationship advice literature. Doctoral dissertation. Retrieved from ProQuest (1696058879)

Ford, G. E. (2012). An investigation of the processes that contribute to African Americans becoming divorced. Doctoral dissertation. Retrieved from ProQuest (1238233182)

Kaufman, D. (2017. The statistical story behind Malia Obama dating a white guy. Retrieved November 28, 2017 from https://quartzy.qz.com/1137956/the-statistical-story-behind-malia-obama-dating-a-white-guy/ King James Version. Holy Bible.

Liu, Nikki. R. (2016). Emerging trends in marriage and systems that impact marital therapy. Doctoral dissertation. Retrieved from ProQuest (1800556807).

Livingston, G. & Brown, A. (2017). Interracial in the U.S. 50 years of Loving v. Virginia/Pew Research Center. Retrieved November 11, 2017 from http://www.pewsocialtrends.org/2017/05/18/intermarriage-in-the-u-s-50-years-after-loving-v-virginia/

Lowndes, L. (1996). *How to make anyone fall in love with you.* New York McGraw-Hill

Pew Research Center (2012). The rise of Interracial Marriage. Retrieved December 15, 2016 from http://www.pewsocialtrends.org/2012/02/16/ the-rise-of-intermarriage/?src=prc-headline

Pew Research Center (2015). Race and social connection—Friends, family and neighborhoods. Retrieved December 15, 2016 from http://www.pewsocialtrends.org/2015/06/11/chapter-5-race-and-social-connections-friends-family-and-neighborhoods/#race-marriage-and-intermarriage

U.S. Census Bureau (2009). Interracial marriages in the United States. Retrieved December 15, 2016 https://en.wikipedia.org/wiki/ interracial_marriage_in_the_United_States

Wikipedia. Anti-miscegenation laws in the United States. Retrieved December 15,2016fromhttps://en.wikipedia.org/ wiki/Antimiscegenation_laws_in_the_United_States

Wright, H. (2006). Female White racial identity in interracial relationships with Black Men: A qualitative study. Doctoral dissertation. Retrieved from ProQuest (304918402)

ABOUT THE AUTHOR

Gabriel Woodhouse is a publisher of The Woodhouse Publishing Post. He publishes books and provides seminars on interracial marriages throughout the U.S.

Gabriel Woodhouse is a graduate of a prestigious institution of higher education. He is a former business writer for a Fortune 500 Company.

Printed in the United States
By Bookmasters